Science and Religion

'Allamah Muhammad Taqi Ja'fari

Translated by
Mansoor Limba

Thoroughly Revised and Edited by
Beytollah Naderlew

Top Ten Award
International Network Inc.

2023

Published by: Top Ten Award International Network Inc.

Vancouver, BC **CANADA**
Email: Info@TopTenAward.Net
www.toptenaward.net

Ordering Information:
Quantity sales. Special discounts are available on quantity purchases by universities, schools, corporations, associations, and others. For details, contact the "Sales Department" at the above mentioned email address.

Science and Religion, 'Allamah Muhammad Taqi Ja'fari, 1st Edition.
ISBN: 978-1-990451-94-2   Paperback

In the Name of Allah,
the All-beneficent, the All-merciful

Contents

Foreword

The question concerning the relationship between religion and reason has long been a subject of inquiry among philosophers, thinkers, theologians, and believers throughout history. However, the inquiry into the relationship between science and religion is a more recent development that emerged in the modern era. While discussions on the relationship between reason and religion in Islamic thought and Western philosophy span over a millennium, the question of the relationship between science and religion arose only a few centuries ago in the Western philosophical context and reached the Islamic world more recently. It is noteworthy that modern science emerged within the framework of the new reason, which encompasses empirical and mathematical reasoning. This form of reasoning was explicitly articulated and defined in the modern era, particularly by philosophers such as Descartes and subsequently by thinkers like Kant.

In the Western world, modern reason and science have had a close interplay, leading to a significant connection between the two. However, religion, particularly Christianity, has not undergone substantial transformation in relation to modern reason and science. Consequently, the claims made by religion regarding the natural world were subjected to scrutiny and challenge by the new reason and modern empirical sciences, primarily in the realm of natural sciences. In contrast, in the Islamic world, the question of the relationship between science and religion has been addressed in a much broader context than in Western Christianity. Islam encompasses diverse areas of inquiry, including ontology, cosmology, anthropology, sociology, and more. Thus, Muslim thinkers have recognized that not only the natural empirical sciences but also the new human empirical sciences pose challenges to and raise questions about Islamic claims. Consequently, they have realized that powerful and prominent rivals, such as modern science, have emerged against religion in the modern era. These rivals not only lack the intention to accompany and be compatible with religion but also strive to exclude religion from the realm of human life.

However, the conflict and struggle between science and religion over the past four centuries in the West have not been constant and uniform, experiencing fluctuations and variations. Some theological inclinations in the West have even moved toward establishing a peaceful and complementary relationship between religion and modern science. In the latter half of the twentieth century, certain trends emerged that aimed to establish a harmonious and even complementary relationship between religion and the new sciences. Nevertheless, in comparison to the West, the Islamic world has less experience and faces more challenges concerning the relationship between the new human sciences and Islam.

Consequently, Muslim thinkers encounter complex and uncharted paths in this regard, and their effective navigation of these paths is crucial to avoiding numerous theoretical and practical dilemmas within the Muslim religious community. Therefore, determining the relationship between the Muslim religious community and the new world necessitates addressing the new sciences that have emerged within the framework of the new reason. This relationship, specifically the relationship between the new sciences and religion, constitutes a scientific hypothesis that requires exploration and examination by the global Muslim community, particularly Muslim intellectuals.

It appears that Muslim thinkers face a demanding and lifelong endeavor, which they embark upon from their youth until the end of their lives. Regarding the subject of science and religion, the works of Allameh Ja'fari can be classified into two levels or categories:

One - General Level: This broad category encompasses a significant portion of Allameh Ja'fari's works pertaining to fields such as cosmology, anthropology, ontology, ethics, and related subjects. These works, particularly evident in his interpretations of Mathnawi and Nahj al-Balagha, offer an exposition of the relationship between the new human sciences and Islamic thought. Within this context, a new form of Islamic human sciences has emerged. In other words, Allameh Ja'fari's works at this general level not only professionally address the discourse on the relationship between the new sciences and religion, especially Islam but also contribute to the production and emergence of novel Islamic human sciences. Therefore, this category of Allameh Ja'fari's scholarly works can be considered as examples of the newly developed Islamic human sciences that have been produced and surfaced.

Two - Specific Level: The second level of discussion concerning the relationship between science and religion in Allameh Ja'fari's works refers to the specific topics that he himself has addressed under the title of "the relationship between science and religion." These are the subjects mentioned in the book.

In conclusion, it is hoped that this collection of discussions on the subject of "science and religion" will be utilized and researched by intellectuals, similar to Allameh Ja'fari's other works.

Allameh Ja'fari's Institute

Science and Religion

Chapter 1
The Relationship of Science, Philosophy, and Religion with Intelligible Life

Science, Religion and Philosophy as the Three Main Elements of Human Intelligible Life

It seems that in order to understand the three great domains of science, philosophy and religion and their relationship with intelligible life, two types of study and research are possible.

First: To examine each one of these triple realities in respect of their nature and salient features in a direct fashion. This is the very popular method which has been used by philosophers and scholars of human sciences since the dawn of such researches till now.

Second: These triple realities have to be assayed in light of a study of ideal form of human life as they all are closely related with a being whose major feature is being a living entity. Then one should first ask what does life mean in this context?

If it means pure natural life, which originates and exists as motivated by natural factors, this kind of life has nothing to do with perfection and goals beyond selfishness; it has nothing to do with justice, humanitarianism, searching for material and spiritual advancements derived from sense of noble duty (beyond egotism). This life does not consider the nobility, and dignity of humanity. This life is harmonious with tangible and intelligible beauties and inclination to them so long as they enhance and make desirable this natural life of man. The fundamental motive in this kind of life is obtrusive selfishness and self-aggrandizement, whereas, the triple realities are all related to the degrees of perfection and sublime aspects of life which we call "intelligible life".

At the beginning of this research, we shall briefly point out the meaning of religion, science and philosophy and then we will delve into them.

I- Religion refers to a set of beliefs, duties and manners without which life would have no basis except obtrusive selfishness — the very selfishness, which the shameful impotence of mankind in controlling it, has made its history unjustifiable. Religion denotes an advanced consciousness in life, knowing it, and moving towards the Absolute Perfection and exposing onself to its divine radiations.

What is religion? Rising up from the face of the dust so that the pure soul may become aware of itself [1]

II. Philosophy signifies knowledge of the foundations of the universe and readiness to answer the questions that goes beyond the corporeal facts that are continuously exposed to change and to be known by positive sciences. The application of this knowledge for the evolutionary becoming of the Self also means wisdom, whose concerns are realities and not conventional concepts, which are based upon individual notions and occasional reasonings.

III. Science consists of discovering realities through observation, experiment and inward perception, or intuition. It is clear that because of the relativity of discovering realities, scientific relation with them is also relative.

It is clear that without religion, science and philosophy, movement along the path of "intelligible life" will be impossible.

What is Intelligible Life?

"Intelligible life" is a kind of life in which all human gifts are being actualized, to the extent possible, to meet his material and spiritual needs. It is the same life described by God:

1. °ay¡tan tayyibah (good life):

> *Whoever acts righteously, [whether] male or female, should he (or she) be faithful — We shall revive him with a good life.*[2]

2. Life by a manifest proof (¡ay¡t 'an bayyinah):

> *... so that he who perishes might perish by a manifest proof, and he who lives may live on by a manifest*

---

1. Mu¡ammad Iqb¡l L¡h£r¢, trans. Arthur J. Arberry, Jaw¡dn¡meh, "D¢n wa Wa§an," lines 1039-1040. [Trans.]
2. S£rat an-Na¡l 16:97.

proof.[1]

3. Real life:

> *O, you who have faith! Answer Allah and the Apostle when he summons you to that which will give you (real) life.*[2]

The point that has been elaborated in the above mentioned verse is that a life without revealed religion is not life at all; rather it is, idiomatically speaking, a caricature of life, which like a volcano may, due to its uncurbed egoism, turn all the farms of human life into soil and put a stamp of heroism on itself!

Whenever the self-defeated ignorant masses find their lives meaningless, they see no clear reason for living, no motives but eating, sleeping, [expressing] anger, and [satisfying] carnal desires. These individuals are pacified by their ego saying that an ideal, organized and law-abiding life is one in which we can satisfy our desires and have no other duty except to avoid disturbing others. Yes, such a life is ideal for them, and for its desirability, we have no need for any reasoning! We have no business with those who do not differentiate between contradictory things.

For these people, ignorance means knowledge; responsible personal freedom equals unrestraint; sensible and intelligible beauty is equivalent to a momentary source of stimulation; justice is synonymous with oppression; law is identical with law violation; life with an understandable identity and of an evolutionary nature is the same as the life of ants and bees. For them, service to humanity, human life and rights is tantamount to utilizing mankind for the urges of the uncurbed natural self, and extermination of mankind and negation of any duty tantamount to the rights of others. Finally, and in sum, being is practically identical with nothingness! This is the requisite of the meaning of the famous statement ingrained in the minds of all 'conscious' individuals: "Everything is possible for anyone who

---

1. Sŧrat al-Anfįl 8:42.
2. Sŧrat al-Anfįl 8:24.

does not believe in God." This latter statement implies that if the life of human beings has no intelligible meaning, not only everything is permissible, but resisting a pleasure which necessitates the extinction of the entire humanity is a genetic disease.

The life whose foundations are grounded on "religion, science and philosophy in the sense of wisdom" enjoys the merits of the highest ideals, which exist in the hearts of the mature Children of Adam ('a). Since the real definition of life is not possible for us, we have no option but to make use of its salient features and merits in order to know it. This is the way to identify every reality, whose essence and identity we are incapable of knowing.

The Salient Features of Intelligible Life

1 - Intelligible life cannot be sacrificed for the means of life: Since "intelligible life" enjoys pure identity, this life would never allow itself to be sacrificed by the self. Let's consider this point very well:

While having a strong desire for what is ideal, man usually plunges into the tools of pleasure when deprived of "intelligible life. This approach pushs real life outside the realm of existence and makes most people experience a sense of futility.

2- The ultimate answerst to the sextuple fundamental questions can only be provided in the "intelligible life" whose three pillars are religion, science and philosophy in the sense of wisdom.

The ultimate answers of the six questions are as follows:

The First Question: Who am I?

We have this highly constructive statement from the Commander of the Faithful ('a): "Whoever knows himself has attained the highest degree of knowledge and gnosis."

Keeping in mind the meaning of this noble statement, if we agree on the real answer to the first question, we will also agree on the answers to the remaining questions above.

We can put the answer to the first question in this manner: I am a creature constituted by various natural elements and a reality, based upon sublime wisdom of God, called the human soul or *nafs*. It makes its entrance into the universe through the channel of nature and in passing through it, with the help of the divine spirit breathed into it, is ready to attain the Supreme Telos of life and gets exposed to the divine radiations of the Absolute Perfection, God, the Glorious. This is a concise answer to the question "Who am I?" in the "Intelligible Life"

The Second Question: Where Have I Come From?

I am a creature with all those faculties and a strong desire to attain the Supreme Telos of life beyond matter and materiality. It is affirmed that out of wisdom and willpower of God, the All-powerful, All-knowing and All-wise, I have been taking a walk on this earth. So, I have come to this world from a world beyond matter.

The Third Question: Where Have I Come?

The answer to the question "Where have I come?" is as follows: I have come to a very meaningful and great working-place which activates the existence of us human beings.

The Fourth Question: Who Am I With?

Our fellow human beings in this world—with whom we interact—would all pass and come into this world through the channel of male-female reproduction. With the principle of division of labor, social life will be ready for us. My fellow human beings also possess everything I have in the natural and supernatural realms. All of us human beings have certain values and the more correctly they are applied in practice, the more harmonious and unified we become. The origin, path and destination of all of us is the same.

The Fifth Question: Where Am I Heading to?

Human existence, with all the amazing physical and spiritual activities it has presented throughout history, has clarified itself for us and also affirmed that the most insignificant phenomenon, behavior, speech, and intentions of man cannot be destroyed without outcome,

> Nothing of a fist of dust would ever be wasted in this tavern
> They make either a pitcher or a barrel or a cup of wine[1]

---

1. Saib Tabrizi.

It is also proved that without Resurrection and eternity, no value, nay no duty or right can be established, and it became clear that

> *The world, galaxy and stars would be a plaything*
>
> *if this long day of the terrestrial had no tomorrow.*[1]

It is established that every wise man, given his balanced mind, can feel the perpetuity of his soul in this life, and inculcate in his mind that the end of this life is not his last station, it then follows, that he will realize "where he is heading".

---

1. N¡¥ir Khusr£, D¡w¡n-e Ash'¡r, Elegy 241.

The Sixth Question: Why Have I Come?

The answer to this question will be completely clarified, for I realize that my existence stems from the sublime wisdom of God, who will never do anything futile. I have great potential which, if activated, will make me attain my lofty goal in life. I can also unmistakably feel a strong desire within me to attain the said lofty goal. The genuineness of this strong desire is as real as all these scientific, technological and artistic advancements. But, the goal one must do his best to attain is to expose oneself to the divine radiations of Absolute Perfection, God. This is the same struggle and searching called "worship" (*'ib¡dah*), in the parlance of religion.

What is worship? After the state of awakening (*yaq"ah*) and the sense of meaningfulness of one's existence in the world, all physical, mental and psychological actions of man are considered acts of worship because it is the moment of feeling that man is in the presence of God. In the sight of God, all the various acts of worship, performance of duty, and observance of human rights are regarded as *dhikr* (remembrance), *tasbīh* (glorification of God), *rukū'* (bowing in prayer), and *sajdah* (prostration) in this vast place of worship (*ma'bad*) which is called the "world" by those who are plunged and immersed in pleasure and futility. Let us closely examine the contents of the following Qur'¡nic verses to not be annihilated by the destructive darkness of ignorance:

> *Soon, We shall show them Our signs in the horizons and in their own souls until it becomes clear to them that He is the Real.*[1]

> *In the earth are signs for those who have conviction and in your own souls [as well]. Will you not then perceive?*[2]

Now, let us scrutinize recorded traditions about knowing one's self. The Commander of the Faithful 'Alī ibn Abī ±¡lib (*'a*)

---

1. S£rat Fu¥¥ilat 41:53.
2. S£rat al-Dh¡riy¡t 51:20-21.

says:

1. "The best of knowledge is knowledge of man and the self."

2. "The best of wisdom is knowledge of the self or identity and appraisal of the self."

3. "The best of wisdom is knowledge of the self. So, whoever knows the self attains wisdom and whoever is ignorant of his self is misguided."

4. "I wonder how a person who is ignorant of his self can know God."

5. "How can a person who is ignorant of his self be able to know others?"

6. "The ultimate ignorance for a person is ignorance of his self."

7. "Whoever knows his self is free from matter and materiality."

8. "Whoever knows his self knows his Lord."

9. "Whoever knows his self attains a lofty station."

10. "Whoever is ignorant of his self is more ignorant of others."

11. "Whoever knows his self is more knowledgeable of others."

12. "Whoever has gnosis of his self attains the highest level of gnosis and knowledge."

13. "Whoever is ignorant of his self strays away from the path of salvation."

Be careful, O seeker of truth! If you want to know the universe as it is, know yourself.

And examine again:

What is religion? Rising from the face of the dust so that the pure soul may become aware of itself [1]

3- Peace of mind, one of the honorable features of "intelligible life" can only be achieved with religion, science and philosophy (in the sense of wisdom). The importance of this merit lies in the fact that in order to cure ailments caused by different types of

---

1. Mu!ammad Iqb¡l L¡h£r¢, trans. Arthur J. Arberry, Jaw¡dn¡meh, "D¢n wa Wa§an," lines 1039-1040. [Trans.]

anxieties, nervousness, apprehensions, and inner contradictions, no expert can think of any remedy except leading an "intelligible life". If humanity had only peacefully led an "intelligible life," only God knows how its shameful history would have turned into something honorable. Because of the disgraceful affliction of most people with spiritual ailments, we have remained incapable of defining man and knowing his real nature!

4- It is only in the realm of the "intelligible life" that the feeling of unity in the performance of duty and observance of rights, human beings, regardless of race, group and nation, attain the highest level of principles and values, which most people still remember. Without taking a step toward the realm of "intelligible life," humanity cannot resist the sword drawn by the wretched bloodthirsty oppressors, such as Cesare Borgia, Machiavelli, Genghis Khan, Nero, Caligula, Tamerlane, and Friedrich Nietzsche[1].

It is within the framework of the "intelligible life" that happiness and sadness, laughter and tears can be understood. As Rumi sings,

Laughter bespeaks of your mercy

Lamentation groans of your anger

These contradictory messages in the world

Refer to the same beloved.[2]

Along the path of the "intelligible life," man is not contented with the natural peculiarities of animalistic life, for as he gets older, he incessantly strives to increase his knowledge and movement toward perfection. Consider the nature of life from the viewpoint of a common individual which is nothing except eating, sleeping, anger, carnal desire, merriment, luxury, and feasting, all animalistic pursuits, and it is clear that the animal has no knowledge of the human status. Thus, it tends not to

---

1. Friedrich Wilhelm Nietzsche (1844-1900): a 19th-century German philosopher and classical philologist who wrote critical texts on religion, morality, contemporary culture, philosophy and science. [Trans.]
2. Rumi's *Divan-e Shams.*

establish any link with the elements of progress and advancement.

Hence, we have to strive to know the nature of life from the viewpoint of a wary person and benefit from his knowledge. We will find that the differences between these two persons are greater than the differences between a human being and a stone! This is because the stone does not make any movement, but the person who spends his life eating and sleeping, is always engaged in struggling against his self that begins high and ends low. The basic peculiarity of the "intelligible life" is that so long as life and death have not reached the lofty station of *"Indeed my prayer and my worship, my life and my death are all for the sake of Allah, the Lord of all the worlds,"*[1] life must go on. This is the meaning of the "good life" (*hay¡t tayyibah*) mentioned in the Qur'¡n.

This merit which must be considered the greatest and most constructive after finding out the answers to the six questions, by means of the "intelligible life", shall be called "curbing egoism". It is an evident phenomenon throughout the history of human life that egoism assumes various forms and has been the source of corruptions, vices, tyranny, and confounding the truth with falsehood. It can be said with confidence that it is possible for all the volcanos on earth and other planets—if ever there are—to become totally inactive or dead but egoism is so ingrained in man's being that it is impossible to uproot it in most people, except by putting an end to their lives! We must say that so long as the vicious disease of egoism is not cured by the "intelligible life" and self-consciousness, called "God-wariness" (*taqw¡*)[2] take its place, all the legal, moral, religious, political and cultural systems desired by human beings, will be like magnificent palaces built on the crater of a volcano.

Any religion, science or philosophy which is incompetent to materialize the "intelligible life" on account of not having the

---

1. S£rat al-An'¡m 6:162.

2 As already mentioned, this key term of Islamic scholarship can be rendered as moral integrity too (Ed.)

abovementioned features of intelligible life cannot do anything positive for mankind, except being used as a tool by profiteers and selfish individuals.

Conclusion

We can draw two very important conclusions from the mutual relationship between religion, science and philosophy:

First: The forms and elements of the "self-preservation" for the management of life cannot undermine the genuineness and immense power of this phenomenon, neither can the tools, elements, forms, and changes in the manifestations and instances of the three basic pillars of the "intelligible life". In the same vein, the difference in environment, conditions and circumstances cannot question whatsoever the genuineness of sound intellection, conscience and intuition.

Second: We human beings have no right to give a final judgment on all issues related to the definition, identity, outcomes, and manifestations of the three great truths because the forms, manifestations and tools of "intelligible life" have different levels and dimensions at all times.

Is there any contradiction between religion, science and philosophy as a means of acquiring wisdom?

"Intelligible life" is not only the ideal life for humankind but it also provides the answer to its problems in all dimensions of life, and it is the only unifying factor of the three great truths, viz. religion, science and philosophy. By "religion" we mean the set of beliefs, obligations, rights, and manners without which life has no foundation except vicious egoism, because of which, man is still contented with the cave-dwelling level of life, inspite of enormous advancement and progress in the expansion of the "cave," the speed of movements and various adornments in it. What we mean by philosophy is no other than wisdom (hikmah), which can take man to the pinnacle of possible perfection with the two wings of knowledge and action.

What is Wisdom?

Wisdom refers to the knowledge of the general foundations

of the universe and preparedness to answer the questions that goes beyond the corporeal facts that are constantly exposed to change (and the function of knowing them is assumed as philosophy (wisdom)). The application of this knowledge in the course of evolutionary becomings of perfection embodies real wisdom that deals with realities and not conventional concepts anchored in subjective understanding and justificative arguments.

Therefore, wisdom refers to the inalterable principles of gnosis (*ma'rifah*) which are not affected by the passage of time, diverse places and various sciences except in their instances, particular points and manifestations. This is while the main issues and principles of "formal" or "official" philosophies are abstractions of their respective periods and certain understandings of man and the world.

In this discourse, we shall mention some examples of the principles of eternal wisdom:

1. The reality of the world is not related to anyone's mental perceptions although there is the interference of the perceiving elements in science, philosophy or any acquired knowledge.

2. The universe has come into being according to the sublime wisdom of God.

3. Every component of the universe subsists according to the law governing it. If there is no law governing the components of the universe, "nothing is a condition for anything" and "at every moment, everything is possible".

4. Man enjoys a high status and noble values and is capable of existential perfection in this universe. The main focus of attention of the philosophers (*hukam¡'*) and mystics (*'uraf¡'*) is for him to achieve the Supreme Telos of life which is higher than his own existence and the world of nature.

> *The deliciousness of milk and honey is the reflection of the (pure) heart: from that heart, the sweetness of every sweet thing is derived.*
>
> *Hence the heart is the substance, and the world is the accident: how should the heart's shadow (reflection) be the object of the heart's*

desire?¹

5. It is an individual and collective obligation of all people to endeavor and struggle for the training and education of this noble creature, and get him prepared to move along the path of "intelligible life".

6. Scientific, intuitive, philosophical, and religious thinking about the universe is one of the primary obligations.

7. Individual relationship with God through the acts of worship is a philosophical necessity.

8. The fundamental beliefs are as follows:

- Belief in the existence of God, the Creator of the universe;
- The Loftiest Attributes of Perfection which solely belong to the Sacred Essence;
- The apostleship (ris¡lah) of the great prophets and [the successorship of] the infallible Im¡ms for the propagation and interpretation of the laws and human rights which emanate from revelation and man's primordial nature;
- Resurrection and eternal life;
- Belief in the leadership of the Messenger of Allah (¥) after the prophets of God and of the infallible Im¡ms ('a) after the Messenger of Allah (¥);

9. Human dignity, honor and nobility that must be completely acknowledged in this life;

10. Responsible freedom;

11. Equality of all before the law;

12. The prescribed rights possessed by all human beings;

13. The criterion of nobility and honor of every person is related to the extent of perfection of his essence (taqw¡);

14. Human beings endowed with the right of a worthwhile and improvable life by God.

These are examples of the basic principles of wisdom as well as those of the religion of God. So, unity and harmony between

---

1. Rumi's *Masnavi*, Book 3, lines 2265-2266, p. 249. [Trans.]

religion and philosophy as a means of wisdom is an axiomatic truth, to deny or doubt which has no basis except ignorance or spite.

Chapter 2
The Definition of Science and Its Characteristics

What is Science?

If something in the mind of a person is totally discovered and is then completely identified, a perception of it is a scientific one; similar to the case of water, which consists of specific elements of oxygen and hydrogen.

Conditions of a Scientific Law

The terms "scientific law," "scientific problem" or "scientific perspective," have diverse meanings. Sometimes, science is meant in its broadest sense to include even scientific theories and hypotheses. This notion can be seen very frequently in recent times. All discourses in theoretical physics, theoretical sociology and other theoretical fields particularly in theoretical social sciences make use of the word "scientific". This is while they are examined for scientific studies and not that they really possess scientific standing. At times, a limited meaning of science is in the sense of an absolute discovery. Science, in its real sense, can determine the destiny and real direction of human life with respect to the four types of relationship, albeit, it is rarely understood in that sense. At present, three conditions of any scientific proposition are given. If we disregard those terms for a while, we will find the same, under different labels.

First Condition: Universality of the Law

In the domain of science, to identify the reality existing in a case, a subject is attributed with a word denoting universality. By doing so, the ambiguity of a subject can be avoided. Instead of the statement "Some substances consist of certain elements of oxygen and hydrogen," the case is presented with a phrase that indicates universality such as "Water as a whole…"

Basis of the Universality of Scientific Propositions

As we have discussed this issue in our *Shinĵkht* (*Knowledge*), pp. 101-107, this basis is of two types:

1) Induction and experimentation of all subjects of the case: For example, all types of animals or all human beings are generally the subject of a scientific proposition such as "All types of animals give birth to their offspring." Of course, direct observation of most types of animals on earth is impossible. Yet, universality can be claimed and a proposition can be brought forth as a scientific one, although this particular negligence must be mentioned for the researchers not to commit any error. Induction and experimentation of all members of a subject is neither possible nor needed. By knowing a subject in terms of its primary elements, we can give general propositions about the members of the subject. When we have learned the nature of water through all its primary elements, we can present it as the subject of a scientific proposition and say that all its members and manifestations with the exception of certain thematic features are such and such; for example, the various salts that are present in water bodies on the surface of the earth. In a nutshell, in order to establish a scientific proposition which encompasses all members of a subject, it is enough to correctly identify the subject. However, while stating a scientific proposition about the types of a genus, knowing the identity of the said genus is not enough; instead, we must investigate every type with all its salient features. For example, by knowing the general genus of animal as a creature with senses which gives birth to its offspring, we cannot have a general knowledge of the identity of the type of animal, such as a horse.

2) Abstract construction: Universality caused by abstract construction means mental activity creates an identity not requiring its manifestations; for example, mathematical numbers and operations, and geometrical problems and theorems. It is true that abstract construction in the minds initially requires actual observations to form number "two"; it is first necessary to see two stones, two persons or two trees, and to form an abstract circle, it is necessary to see a round vessel or container. However, after undergoing the initial stages, constructing the said identities does not require actual observations. It is for this reason that their generality is realized through the activity of mental construction. To conclude that four plus four equals eight $(4 + 4 = 8)$ in normal mature minds does not require seeing a single case. Thus, if we assume that development of a mind is possible without undergoing the initial stages of observations, mathematical operations will also be possible without any contact with objective realities. In addition, in the process of mathematical operations, the human mind does not pay any attention to actual manifestations, which are the origin of abstraction of the units of those operations.

Generalization of a Scientific View

The universality of a proposition is required for the validity of a scientific law. We can explain the place of mind vis-à-vis a subject in a scientific process thus:

I. Mental preparedness to perceive a subject as motivated by factors we have explained in the first discourse. For this preparedness, one must keep in mind the essential conditions of the mind and the obstacles that may stand in the way of establishing a connection between the mind and the subject. For example, if the mind of the researcher does not regard as scientifically achievable a subject which it wants to identity scientifically, this perception about the subject is a mental obstacle that occupies a certain level of the researcher's mind and he has no option but to remove this obstacle first. For instance, in order to have an inclination to scientifically perceive a subject, a logical motive is definitely essential and without such a motive, the relationship between the mind and the subject will be superficial, and there will be no outcome except imagination and baseless suppositions.

II. In sustaining the duration of relationship, there must always be a kind of implicit mental activity, of which the researcher may possibly not be aware. We can call this activity proposition-formulation. For example, in studying an animal, we encounter tens of phenomena, movements and relations, each of which exists within the framework of specific laws. In other words, what we mean by investigation of animal-under-discussion is only the reaction of its member vis-à-vis heat. Thus, in order to realize this purpose, we can see the speed of the movements of the animal. Moreover, we can identify the fast from the slow movement. Meanwhile, we can also discern the reason behind those two types of movements although our main purpose is neither to identify the types of movement nor to discern the reason behind them. Yet, consciously or unconsciously, two types of proposition-formulation exist in our minds:

One is that one movement is faster than another, or this movement is slower than that movement. The other is that the reason behind the fast movement is the intense effect of the desire to escape which prompts the animal to move faster.

III. Benefiting from this mental law that the phenomenon which appears as an effect in the actual world shall definitely appear again with the repetition of the cause because this effect is not a phenomenon exclusive to the individual in the actual world. So, one must engage in abstraction and experimentation and scrutinize this effect in different conditions and circumstances.

IV. If, by means of an all-embracing abstraction and experimentation, we can arrive at a general proposition applicable to all cases, we will find out the general law governing those cases. Universality of the fourth stage is abstracted from the scientific relationship with the subject while all the cases prior to the fourth stage are essential for the commencement of a scientific course.

V. When a general law is arrived at by means of abstractions and experimentations, a number of phenomena will also be presented as conditions and obstacles to the purport of the law.

Second Condition: Conditional Predictability

Since every event in the factual world depends on certain conditions as well as the absence of impediments, the scientific laws which are grounded on those happenings are conditional, whether those conditions are explicitly stipulated in the text of the law, or not. We know that whenever the earth is situated between the sun and the moon, an eclipse will occur. This law depends on two conditions. One is that there must be no change to take place in the solar system. The other is that the earth must be situated between the sun and the moon. Given these two conditions, we can predict the occurrence of a lunar eclipse one night in the future. In the same manner, the placement of the earth between the sun and the moon is also a predictable phenomenon, given specific conditions. Of course, since this second condition bespeaks of the conformity of law with reality, this is not exclusive to the prediction of a future occurrence. By taking into account the identity of the law with all its conditions, we can also acquire scientific information of the past as well as the present. We say, for example, that pieces of evidence show that six months ago, the earth was situated between the sun and the moon for two hours. Therefore, we arrive at the definite conclusion that six months ago, a lunar eclipse occurred for two hours. Similarly, if the said condition exists now, then there is definitely a lunar eclipse.

Third Condition: Refutability

Refitability means inconsistency of a scientific proposition with all the possible phenomena. It is for this reason that it is said, "No scientific proposition is indifferent vis-à-vis all the phenomena in the world.

It seems that it is quite erroneous for researchers to set this third condition against the second condition and to present them as two separate conditions. This is because when a proposition is advanced in the form of a general law, it is not an abstract and indivisible truth. It is rather the subject of law, which can be scrutinized elaborately, and its predicate and the relationship between the subject and the predicate depend on certain conditions and the absence of obstacles. These components, limitations and conditions have their respective contributions in the materialization of the law, just as by their materialization in a certain condition, one can acquire scientific information on the materialization of the purport of law. In the same manner, with the minimum absence of those components, limitations and conditions, one can also consider definite the inability of the purport of the law to be materialized. For example, let us analyse this law: "Every wise man is useful for his society."

The subject of this law can be broken down or analyzed as follows:

- man;
- His rational and conscientious maturity up to the degree of wisdom; and
- His readiness to make use of his wisdom in society;

The predicate of this law can be broken down as follows:

- The existence of society which accommodates wise activities;
- The types of existing usefulness, the most suitable of which the wise person makes use of or acts upon for society; and
- Social disorders stand in the way of acceptance of the usefulness of the wise person.

It is obvious that for the actual materialization of the usefulness of the wise person in society, the abovementioned conditions and the absence of obstacles are essential. As a result, we can predict the materialization of usefulness as a legal phenomenon with the abovementioned conditions. At the same time, we have to accept that with the absence of one of them such usefulness shall be invalid and not be materialized as a legal phenomenon. If all the abovementioned items are present but due to inner or outward defects, the wise person is not prepared to have a wise activity in his society, the said law lacks the required condition.

Fourth Condition: Repeatablity and Duplicablity

If the subject under consideration is an unrepeatable and unmultipliable reality, it cannot be studied from the scientific point of view. Take, for example, the case of a work of art. Considering the motive of the artist and his work's identity and manifestations, it can be repeated in no time and conditions. In this case, this work cannot be scientifically studied because it is

a particular and specified phenomenon that cannot be the basis
of abstraction of a general law or a case for conformity with the
general law. As a result, studying the entire universe as a single
unit, which cannot be repeated and multiplied, at least for us, it
is beyond the scientific domain. In the same manner, studying
the Essence and Being of God (not the principle of His existence),
which can neither be repeated nor multiplied is a subject beyond
science.

In addition to the explanation and argument we have given,
this is a condition for a scientific proposition. The important
point that must be emphasized here is that in the concrete and
abstract world, no phenomenon can really be repeated or
multiplied, and whatever is materialized is subjective, and in the
parlance of logic, a real particular which it is impossible to repeat
and multiply.

What we call "repetition" is a similar or parallel occurrence of
phenomena in the concrete and abstract world. In reality, this
occurrence is similar to that of the rays of light which because of
their similarity in nature seem to be recurring, whereas in reality,
the rays of light can never occur again or be multiplied. It must,
therefore, be said that one of the conditions of a scientific
proposition is that it is indicative of the occurrence of similar or
parallel things in the world of realities. In fact, in a sense, we can
say that the comparative similarities are not pecfect, for in the
words of Mawlawī (Rūmī),

> This abode (the world) does not contain any form (that is) one (with
> any other form), so that I might show forth to you a similitude.
>
> Still, I will bring to hand an imperfect comparison that I may
> redeem your mind from confusion.[1]

Thus it has been clearly shown that the only way through
which one can expose oneself to the divine radiations of the
Absolute Perfection is intelligible life. The issue of the nature and
characteristics of religion shall be dealt with after the debate on
science was wrapped up. Let's now turn to the false claims of the

---

1. Rumi's *Masnavi*, Book 4, lines 423-424, p. 51. [Trans.]

conflict between religion, philosophy and science.

The Jugglers' Display of the Alleged Conflict among Science, Religion and Philosophy

The previous debate proves the artificiality of the so-called conflict among religion, science and philosophy in the sense of wisdom. Now, we shall identify those who are responsible for displaying the said alleged conflict. It seems that there are some groups responsible for this baseless display of conflict, and there is only one group which really strives hard to find out the truth.

The *first group* refers to those who earn much pleasure in kindling the fire of conflict among people, especially among thinkers. Sometimes, the weapons in this confrontation are religion, science and philosophies, and at other times, political, cultural financial issues and problems.

The *second group* refers to those who kindle the fire of disputes among people, especially among experts, for social fame and an unwise goal. Therefore, let us assume that if the time comes when this group fails to create baseless conflict, they will conceive of other issues to create disagreements. It is the same work done by David Hume[1] and his followers!

The *third group* can be those who, without paying attention to the subject of dispute and without having knowledge of the existing cases pertaining to the subject, are willing to become tools in the hands of the contenders, expressing their views on the subject though totally ignorant of it! In social gatherings and sometimes even in universities around the world, such simple-minded individuals are needed to express an opinion about issues pertaining to social sciences, political schools of thought and parties. Such individuals can be utilized a lot, and it is possible that the subordinates of groups in such issues would

---

1. David Hume (1711-1776), Scottish historian and philosopher, who influenced the development of skepticism and empiricism, is considered one of the greatest skeptics in the history of philosophy. Hume thought that one's subjective perceptions never provide true knowledge of reality and one can know nothing outside of experience. Accordingly, even the law of cause and effect was an unjustified belief. [Trans.]

utilize such helpless individuals as lifeless tools.

> *Turn to the humble people for help/ As these men are the wings of others despite having their own wings broken.* [1]

The *fourth group* consists of the modernists who exploit the notion of modernism (innovation and progress), which is so constructive, and they never want to exert efforts. In this regard, they suppose, for example, that the concept of time — millions of years ago, this very moment, or millions of years from now — has no concrete reality whatsoever because, accordingly, time is nothing but a mental spatium abstracted from motion — be it inward or outward. What is real is that the gradual increase of the creatures and phenomena in the plain of existence requires the spatium of motion that leads to the abstraction of time in the human mind. Modernism and innovation is not only so good but also, a necessity for the human mind, non-observance of which leads to stagnancy and man's detachment from the inward and outward reality of the concrete world. This principle of modernism is not only related to the essence of time, which allegedly has no concrete reality, but, we benefit from the abstraction of time as the conventional way of measuring the amount of increase of a temporal creature.

The *fifth group* consists of the truth-seekers who want to acquire information about the subjects of dispute and know the truth. Their efforts along this line only mean to know the reality under contention. In fact, as much as they can, they want to make use of that reality for themselves and other members of society. In this regard, one can cite the important views of some contemporary experts:

> *The anxiety of the sensitive minds, the ardent desire to know the truth and discern the importance of a subject, must stir in us the most sincere feeling of sympathy. Whenever we consider the supposed functions of religion and science, we will see that it is not an exaggeration for us to regard the future trend of history*

---

1. Saib Tabrizi.

as dependent on the decision of the present generation on the quality of relations between the two (religion and science). Here, we are facing two powers, the most formidable of all, and these two are different from the stimulation caused by our five senses and which influences human personality. But it is as if they oppose one another: one draws us to religious intuition while the other is that force which draws us toward exploratory observation as well as logical induction.[1]

Any conceptual issue which can be erroneous in social sciences may possibly be susceptible to Machiavellian political abuse, especially that which pertains to religion, science and philosophy, which have been encompassed by unscientific motives, and in particular, by political agenda in recent times.

If the state of affairs in our time were such that the study and research about religion and science were conducted with utmost neutrality, and were without motives caused by the vices of selfishness, domination, an important step would have been taken in knowing the real relationship between religion and science, and their excellent cooperation for man's attainment of felicity. Unfortunately, however, states of affairs exactly in opposition to this purity, sincerity and love for the truth can be observed. Nowadays, anybody or any group which has more material power by means of acquiring means and tools of media propaganda and technological prowess has more chance of achieving their objectives. They can utilize all means of domination in order to bring home their claims and to infuse and impose whatever they like to the simple-minded communities. They have sophisticated skill in handling artificial and irrational disputes and conflicts. The following points are worthy of note:

1. At the time of breaking down creatures into their component parts—including natural things, machines, and any man-made product or mental conception—we do not go into the detail of time which we conventionally divide into second, minute, hour, and the like. For example, when dismantling a

---

1. N¡meh-ye Farhang, vol. 1, no. 3, p. 21.

machine or demolishing a factory—although it supposedly took fifteen years from the time of manufacturing or building it up to the time of its dismantlement or demolition—even a second from the said fifteen years cannot be found in it as a concrete entity.

2. In a certain magazine, there is an article by A. Bultman with this title:

> Science for Sale or Experts at the Service of Technology and Politics.[1]

3. An article by Schmidt Hals has the following title:

> Wrong Attitude of Researchers: A Study of Vital Medical Research Works in Comparing the Laws in Two Currently Advanced Countries.[2]

4. A three-page article by Dirg Furger in the same magazine has this title:

> The Researcher as Fraud in Science.[3]

5. A two-page article by Prof. Von Whitsku is entitled "Wrong Understandings of the Views of Darwin."[4]

6. A book entitled "A Collection of Interesting Errors for the Public," mentions 500 errors that include direct or indirect scientific errors. This book is written in 1996 by two German professors named Walter Kremer and Guts Turnker and it is one of the second prize winners.[5]

7. A book titled "How Science Was at Fault" written by Herman Armin, a German author of the history of science.[6]

8. Murray Gell-Mann, winner of the Noble Prize in Physics in 1969 said, thus: "That there has been much delay in presenting the suitable philosophical explanation to quantum (physics) is because of the fact that Neils Bohr[7] said,

---

1. Bilderwind Erkentinis (1994), no. 2.
2. Ibid.
3. Ibid. (1996).
4. Ibid.
5. Ibid. (1996), no. 11.
6. Wie die Wissenxchaft Ihre Unschuld Verlor (Germany), 1981.
7. Niels Henrik David Bohr (1885 – 1962): a Danish physicist who received the Nobel Prize in Physics in 1922, and his son, Aage Bohr (who grew up to be an

Everything in explaining quantum mechanics of the past 50 years has been done already.[1]

Notwithstanding his indisputable prominence and high reputation in science, Bohr was not supposed to deceive humanity with the false nature of science, which the Machiavellians try to utilize in different societies.

How do those, who present an artificial contradiction between religion, science and philosophy, explain the existence of such personalities as Socrates, Plato, Aristotle, Muḥammad ibn ±urkhᵢn Fᵢrᵢbī, Abū 'Alī ibn Sīnᵢ, Abū Rayhᵢn Bīrūnī, Ibn Rushd, Khwᵢjah Na¥īr al-Dīn al-±ūsī,[2] Jalᵢl al-Dīn Muḥammad Mawlawī (Rūmī), 'Abd al-Rahmᵢn ibn Khaldūn, Descartes,[3] Leibniz,[4] Helmholtz,[5] Max Planck, Albert Einstein, and Weizsäcker,[6] and hundreds of others?

In fact, according to Max Planck in his book *Where is Science Going?*,

Great thinkers of all ages have been religious men although they may not have feigned religiosity.[7]

---

important physicist) in 1975. [Trans.]

1. Bilderwind Erkentinis (1996), no. 6.

2. Muḥammad ibn Muḥammad ibn °asan al-±£¢, better known as Khwᵢjah Na¥ir al-D¢n al-±£¢ (597-672 AH/1200-73): a Persian polymath and prolific writer—an astronomer, biologist, chemist, mathematician, philosopher, physician, physicist, scientist, theologian, and marja' al-taql¢d (religious authority). [Trans.]

3. René Descartes (1596-1650): French mathematician and the founding father of modern philosophy. His theory of knowledge starts with the quest for certainty, for an indubitable starting-point or foundation on the basis alone of which progress is possible. This is eventually found in his celebrated 'Cogito ergo sum' which means "I think therefore I am." [Trans.]

4. Gottfried Wilhelm Leibniz (1646 – 1716): a polymath German philosopher and mathematician who wrote in multiple languages, primarily in Latin (~40%), French (~30%) and German (~15%). [Trans.]

5. Hermann Ludwig Ferdinand von Helmholtz (1821 – 1894): a German physician and physicist who made significant contributions to several widely varied areas of modern science. [Trans.]

6. Carl Friedrich Freiherr von Weizsäcker (1912 – 2007): a German physicist and philosopher. [Trans.]

7. Max Planck, 'Ilm beh Kujᵢ Mᶜrawad? (Where is Science Going?), trans. Aḥmad ᵢrᵢm, p. 235 (originally in Persian).

Is It Science or Chicanery?

Stanislav Andreski, a professor of sociology at the University of Reading, United Kingdom, has written a book entitled *"Social Sciences and Sorcery"* (1972), in which he accuses the majority of social scientists of pretentious and nebulous verbosity, interminable repetition of platitudes and disguised propaganda. At least 95 per cent of research is indeed re-search for things found long ago and many times since. Without dwelling on general points, he substantiates his claims. He accuses Talcott Parsons, known to be the father of modern sociology, of "extreme vagueness," saying that he presents "the simplest of truth as an incomprehensible, intricate problem." That which particularly irritates Andreski is Parsons' "voluntaristic theory of action".

In a nutshell, "Translated from the tenebrous language in which it is couched, this theory amounts to saying that in order to understand why people act as they do, we must take into account their wishes and decisions, the means at their disposal and their beliefs about how the desired effects can be produced." As Andreski mockingly comments, "The emergence of this piece of knowledge amounted, no doubt, to an important step in the mental development of mankind, but it must have occurred some time during the Paleolithic Age, as Homer and the Biblical prophets knew all about it."

In the same way, Andreski also criticizes other prominent scholars such as Paul Lazarsfeld,[1] his colleague and the famous author of the controversial book entitled *"Personal Influence"*. Regarding him, Andreski says, "After painstakingly studying a plethora of tables and formulas, we will reach the point of a common discovery (which is, of course, expressed in the most intricate way) that individuals earn pleasure in drawing others' attention. Or, a person is under the influence of those whom he interacts with… Of course, these are axiomatic points which my

1. Paul Felix Lazarsfeld (1901 – 1976): one of the major figures in 20th-century American sociology and the founder of Columbia University's Bureau of Applied Social Research. [Trans.]

grandmother used to mention during my childhood."

Another famous figure who is subjected to criticism is Skinner,[1] the Harvard University professor, who, according to Andreski, has seriously misinterpreted human nature, and by advancing forth the most trivial subject "real portrait of the human mind," he encourages irresponsibility and nihilism, which ultimately "turns influential in the social lives of people".

Without disregarding the importance of their works in promoting fundamental self-consciousness in real life's situations, Andreski describes Freud, Adler[2] and Jung with most respect, as devoid of "the sense of coherence and proportionality. And in his conclusion from the research findings of such scholars, he writes, "We linger on the vacuum between quantitative vulgarities and flight in the pleasant worlds, though devoid of order and rule."

The most important source of concern by Andreski are these "quantitative vulgarities" which can be regarded as one of the distinctive features of social sciences. In his opinion, the truly important human traits can never be measured, and most of those that can, are inconclusive.

In criticizing the experts in behavioral sciences, Andreski points out that by using "quasi-mathematical arrangements," they portray their works as "scientific" and one is astonished as to what expression he must have. For example, Claude Lévi-Strauss,[3] a famous anthropologist, describes the distinction between two animals by the equation "panther = ant-eater". If this formula is expressed in its mathematical meaning, the meaning of the statement is as follows: a panther is equivalent to the number "one" divided by "ant-eater" whose outcome is nothing but, witnessing the magical light of fiction and seeing its

1. Burrhus Frederic Skinner (1904 – 1990): an American behaviorist, author, inventor, social philosopher and poet. [Trans.]
2. Alfred Adler (1870 – 1937): an Austrian medical doctor, psychotherapist, and founder of the school of individual psychology. [Trans.]
3. Claude Lévi-Strauss (1908 – 2009): a French anthropologist and ethnologist, and has been called, along with James George Frazer, the "father of modern anthropology". [Trans.]

various colors, one would get melancholic.

Another example, extracted from mathematics and used by numerous sociologists, is the letter "n" which is "so melancholic". This letter represents the word "need" used by David McClelland,[1] Harvard University professor of psychology to portray different needs, and Andreski sarcastically says that for reading this subject, man has a new "need" called "prevalence of chicanery".

Andreski, by mentioning the names of social scientists, accuses them of hardly dedicating themselves to the search for truth and being more attached to money, fame and recognition. Of course, given the method they have adopted, they could attain their desire at once. According to him, in social sciences "there are dim-witted and low-educated individuals who become aware that they can be known as researchers and professors". Then, to actually prove his claim, Andreski gave a philological examination to social sciences students in Great Britain and proved that "these students, compared to other students, including those of engineering and physics, would get lower marks"! Andreski's goal in publishing the book is to warn readers to be very meticulous in reading such works and not be deceived by the conventional pleonasm, formulas, tables, and discoveries of the "high-ranking" writers.[2]

---

1. David C. McClelland (1917 – 1998): an American psychological theorist noted for his work on achievement motivation as reflected in a number of his writings from the 1950s until the 1990s. [Trans.]
2. Stanislav Andreski, "Social Sciences and Sorcery" as translated [into Persian] by the esteemed and learned friend Muḥammad Jawịd Sahlịnẹ, Iqti¥ịd wa Andẹsheh Journal.

Chapter 3
Stability and Change in Science and Religion

Can stability and change in science and religion mean the same?

In one of the most substantial articles by "Alfred North Whitehead," the author maintains that both religion and science have dimensions of stability and change. Since each of them belongs to a different realm, the fusion of these two dimensions in religion does not lead to contradiction. These two dimensions are as follows:

1. General principles and basic foundations of religion and science which are inalterable truths, and

2. The manifestations of those inalterable truths and the quality and quantity of the understanding about them

At the outset, we should remind the reader of a very important distinction between religion and science, which is that change in religion is based upon the changes that take place in the manifestations of laws, religious duties and rights, but not in the religious laws, duties and rights themselves. For example, prior to the emergence of technological advancements in human societies, if the movement from one point to another—let us say, for transporting goods or for religious travels such as journey to Mecca—by means of four-footed animals is incumbent, after the emergence of technological advancements, movement or transportation through advanced means of transportation will become incumbent. So is the case of agricultural machineries, industrial machines, different methods of business transaction, modes of training and education, performance of the acts of worship, etc.

The inalterable and general principles of the abovementioned matters never undergo any changes; for example, preservation of decent life, establishing connection with God, and subsistence on the basis of ardent desire for perfection which leads to the acquisition of taqw¡ (God-wariness or protection of the self from pollutions and impurities). This is while the accidental changes and transformations in any branch of science lead to the transformation of the said branch. This is because the nature of science implies understanding of the actual realities by means of sensory perceptions, mental activities, experimental activities, and other intensive and extensive ways. It is clear that even this understanding, discovery, affirmation, and negation are in the process of change. This is while the real essence of religion is different from the understanding and interpretation of the textual sources and references of religion, although perception of the principles of religion becomes possible through understanding and knowing it from its textual sources and references.

Notwithstanding the differences arising from the variety and limitation of viewpoints, devices, and orientations in the realm of science, it is totally clear that sometimes, by means of sensory perceptions, intellection and other modes of communication, we are more meticulous in their complete discovery. Without doubt, such connection with the world of nature and its manifestations—if it is not the best—is certainly one of the best ways of connecting with them. Our main problem, however, is that this way of establishing connection with the realities of the universe is very limited and insufficient in comparison to what we can be able to know. If man, from the beginning of his life on planet earth, would have been contented with the little information he could acquire through the limited means and considered "science" whatever he could see with his eyes or perceive with the other senses, he could not have made any progress in science, technology and social sciences. Therefore, man cannot rely only on his limited observations, he cannot imprison himself within the state of cave-dwelling.

If the prominent scholars had pondered on the inner forces and mental factors that made them strive hard to understand the causes, conditions and impediments of phenomena, our scientific and civilizational advancements would have been beyond description. If such men of ideas as Ibn Sīnī would have contented themselves only with their observations about the "four elements"[1] called water, fire, earth, and wind, that they could observe, could the identification and elaboration of all the main elements in the Mendeleev[2] Table (or the periodic table of the chemical elements) be possible?

We have to point out that in this discourse we will take Islam as the model, being the culmination of the Abrahamic faiths, Christianity, Judaism, Zoroastrianism, Sabeanism, and even those religions, which share general principles and fundamental beliefs with the Abrahamic Creed.

The most common and fundamental principle which all Abrahamic Faiths adhere to is the principle to which God has ordered the Holy Prophet (¥) to invite the followers of all religions so as to have a common platform of actions:

> Say, 'O People of the Book! Come to a word common between us and you: that we will worship no one but Allah, and that we will not ascribe any partner to Him, and that we will not take each other as lords besides Allah'. But if they turn away, say, 'Be witnesses that we are muslims'.[3]

The truths we will set forth as inalterable principles of religion are traceable to the principle of tawhīd (Oneness of Allah) and negation of any partner for Him:

I. General Principles and Inalterable Fundamentals of Religion

The existence of God implies these general principles:

1. God, the Glorious, who is perfect, self-sufficient, all-

---

1. According to the cosmology of Aristotle (384-322 BCE) as expounded in his On the Heavens and Physics, the universe or cosmos is divided into the earthly or sublunary region and the heavens. In the sublunary region, substances are made up of the four elements, viz. earth, water, air, and fire. See Aristotle, "Physics and On the Heavens," in Jonathan Barnes (ed.), The Complete Works of Aristotle: The Revised Oxford Translation (Princeton: Princeton University Press, 1984). [Trans.]

2. Dmitri Ivanovich Mendeleev (1834 – 1907): a Russian chemist and inventor credited as being the creator of the first version of the periodic table of elements. [Trans.]

3. Sɛrat ¡l 'Imr¡n 3:64.

knowing, all-powerful, and all-wise, has created the universe based on wisdom and good purpose.

2. It is impossible for a human being to occupy a lofty status and nature without the goal he must achieve through correct training, learning and searching. Negation of the lofty goal of human life is tantamount to the waiving of all human principles and values as well as negation of the wisdom and bounty of God.

3. Man can know God in two ways. The first is by observing the orderliness of the external universe, the motion of matter, the choice of a particular path of motion, and the emergence of the phenomenon of life from matter, and observing the celestial world through advanced technology. The second is the inward way of man's pure nature and clear intuition. The advantage the inward way has over the outward way is that this way actualizes the manifestation of God in man's being.

4. Without accepting the Day of Resurrection and eternal life, no principle and value can ever be established by man. All the self-sacrifices in the way of reforming the individual and society done on the basis of values cannot be analyzed and interpreted as anything other than imprudence of the highest order by those who do not believe in the above!

5. Performance of acts of worship is essential if one is to expose oneself to the divine radiations of the Absolute Perfection although religions differ with each other with regards to the quantity and quality of these acts of worship. There is no phenomenon similar to the acts of worship for this life-giving philosophy of exposing oneself to the radiations of Absolute Perfection.

6. Human beings are obliged to do good deeds, whose criterion is the material and spiritual welfare of the people.

7. Human beings must observe the rights of individuals and groups in society as well as maintain proper management. In the same manner, they must also give utmost importance to the observation of their own rights. Therefore, just as individuals are not supposed to harm others, they are equally not supposed to harm themselves, physically and spiritually. From the religious

perspective, no person is allowed to corrupt himself being free, commit suicide, undermine his honor and dignity, or commit any sin.

8. The movement anchored in justice, equity and fairness is always at loggerheads with the selfishness of the powerful, hedonists and lascivious, so, without God's order to initiate this movement, no guarantee for its realization can be given. As such, religion is needed to give meaning to these matters. The following point brought forth by Jean-Jacques Rousseau bespeaks of an eternal truth concerning the physical and spiritual nature of man. He says,

> In order to discover the best laws which are useful to the nations, there is a need for the Universal Intellect that knows all human desires but has no desire of Its own (i.e. not corrupted by any desire) and has no relation at all with nature (i.e. immune from its contamination) while knowing it very well. Its felicity should not be related to us but is willing to help us attain felicity… Accordingly, only the gods could duly bring out laws for the people.[1]

9. Religion can never limit itself to organizing the social life of individuals although it is one of its functions. Proper organization of social life through rights and laws is one of the most important elements in preparing society to benefit from religion.

10. The great prophets and their rightful successors and executors of will have two divine stations and designations: One is to propagate the laws, duties and rights set by God on the basis of revelationreceived by the prophets. The other is the supervision and management of society.

Revolutionary societies are constantly in need of a great leader in order to protect the revolution from corruption and decadence. In the same manner, in order to preserve the fundamentals of the advanced laws, duties, rights and morality

---

1. Jean-Jacques Rousseau, Social Contract, trans. Ghul¡m-°usayn Z¡rakz¡deh, 3rd printing, p. 81 (originally in French).

of society, a religious society is constantly in need of a leader with excellent skills in social management and whose orders are accepted because he qualifies as a religious leader.

11. The implementation of laws that are wholesome and called "moral precepts"is essential. In contrast to some social and philosophical schools, whose acceptability is natural and conventional, the bedrock of morality in religion is the will and wisdom of God. Religion has set forth inalterable laws, rights and duties whose origins are permanent needs of man; for example, the acts of worship and the prohibition of whatever is physically and spiritually harmful to man.[1]

II. The Ever-Changing Variables in Religion

General manifestations are expressions of inalterable truths stemming from the pure and permanent needs of human beings.

From a broader perspective, we must say that the religion of Islam is "adherent" in harmonizing life with the above items (general subjects, cases and manifestations) except in cases of the acts of worship such as prayer, fasting, and the like. Islam considers whatever increases man's knowledge and dominance over the world of nature and has a role to play in preparing the means to a wholesome life (i.e. intelligible life), as essential and obligatory to utilize. For example, different kinds of medical treatment, putting up educational institutions (from primary school to university) and laboratories, means of transportation, technological devices whose outputs are essential and useful for a wholesome life. Regarding products, which bring about physical and spiritual harm to man, such as, narcotics drugs and other harmful substances, Islam has no positive view about them and wages a serious campaign to uproot them.

III. General Principles and Inalterable Foundation of Science

Like religion, science has a set of general and fundamental

---

1. For detailed information about the alterable and inalterable variables in religion, see Muḥammad Taqī Ja'farī, Tarjumeh wa Tafsīr-e Nahj al-Balīghah, vol. 24, pp. 243-308.

principles which are inalterable and are not open to changes and modification in their nature, some of which are as follows:

1. Following a scientific proposition with sound sensory perceptions to the extent necessary;

2. The senses, because of the limitation, specifics and conditions of their activity, only show the truth within the scope of their perception and give conclusions according to the existing conditions and circumstances.

Some argue,

> It is true that we cannot have real knowledge of the things per se through our natural senses, structural peculiarities, and temporal and spatial standpoints, but very accurate instruments (microscope, telescope) which have been made for extensive and intensive studies in science can facilitate our connection with reality.

It is true that those instruments render us significant help in establishing connection with realities, but they cannot decrease the limitations of our understanding. From the ultimate perspective of science, even if the existing instruments become more accurate, still they cannot show us reality as it is. This is because every instrument has its own limitations and cannot show all dimensions of reality. For this reason, the leading philosophers of the East, especially the Muslim philosophers, have a consensus of opinion that we do not have the capability of real knowledge (ultimate point), and as human beings, our task is to know things by their most distinctive features. ¯adr al-Muta'allihīn Shīrjzī (Mullj ¯adrj) categorically defines philosophy as "the knowledge of the truths, to the extent possible and feasible to man".

3. The universe which science is supposed to discover has an external reality and is not a product of our thinking.

4. It is true that the manner of scientific connection with things depends on the orientation, willpower and inclination of human beings. For example, in the world of nature, there are very important forces and man can identify those forces through

scientific ways and utilize them for the realization of his goals. But, whether these forces can be utilized to organize and reform his life or to annihilate him depends on his choice. Unfortunately, concerning this choice made by man, no anthropologist worth his name can talk without being embarrassed. It is clear that science is bereft of values, it can never pay attention to the cries of those who are weltering in their own blood in the cities and deserts or, the violation of the rights of the weak, except when observing those rights is deemed a value in science.

5. The scientific movement is embedded in man's nature without which man's stagnation is not only definite but it also necessitates retrogression. What is more important is that knowledgeable and gifted individuals with a conscience, scientific consciousness, dedication, and a sense of responsibility should manage the benefits of scientific discoveries. Without this management, historical suicide is the definite outcome predicted in the Vancouver Conference[1] by the prominent scholars of the world.

IV. Change and Development in Science in the Course of Time

Here, we shall quote one of the greatest scientific figures in contemporary time. Alfred North Whitehead, known to most scientists and philosophers says, "Science is even more variable than theology. No scientist can accept the views of Galileo,[2] Newton[3] and even scientific views of the past ten years as inalterable and non-modifiable." Therefore, the difference in

---

1. For a detailed analysis of the declaration issued at the end of this conference see, M. T. Jafari (2014), Human Universal Rights, trans. Beytollah Naderlew.
2. Galileo Galilei (1564-1642): an Italian physicist, mathematician, astronomer, and philosopher who played a major role in the Scientific Revolution by supporting Copernicanism, among many others. [Trans.]
3. Isaac Newton (1643-1727): an English physicist, mathematician, astronomer, natural philosopher, alchemist, and theologian whose best-known discoveries are the laws of motion and universal gravitation as expounded in his 1687 magnum opus Philosophiæ Naturalis Principia Mathematica (usually called the Principia). [Trans.]

interpreting religious sources must not be deemed a justification to undermine the firmness of its general principles and whatever stems from the permanent needs of man.

Apart from religion and science, not all the interpretations of the intellect ('aql)—in spite of having correct axiomatic principles and essential propositions—are also acceptable to the authorities.

Chapter 4

The Relationship of Science and Philosophy with Metaphysics

One of the most significant issues in the realm of science is that without taking the existence of transcendental realities for granted, scientific matters will never know the realities which man is by his nature so eager to know. There are numerous reasons for this:

1. The interference of the elements of perception on the "perceived thing". These elements of perception include the natural senses of man and extremely advanced instruments essential for the extensive and intensive knowledge of the realities in the universe.

2. The goals of a researcher who definitely strives hard to know the dimensions of things.

3. The relationship of all creatures with one another admits that if there are unknown among them, it is enough that it is impossible to know them.

The combination of the first and second elements makes this immortal saying, "In the great stage play of existence, we are both performers and spectators," to be recognized as the most correct principle about knowledge since the time of the Chinese philosopher Laozi.

4. Ancient philosophers, both in the East and the West, have acknowledged that we do not know the real nature of things; rather, our knowledge is a product of logical differentia and genera, which are special merits of things over one another.

5. One can say that all experts with a profound worldview will become aware of the problem of knowing the realities when they confess this with utmost perspicacity and intellectual humility. In order to explain and prove this confession, we shall quote some statements of contemporary scholars and

philosophers.

Here we shall examine the views of the most famous Eastern and Western philosophers about "the essence of the natural world". Needless to say, we should have quoted them directly so as to substantiate the matters discussed here. The quotations sometimes include other issues other than those related to "the essence of the natural world" which may be unacceptable to us. Thus, the readers must bear in mind that quoting statements that include those issues does not mean accepting them, because our purpose, as we have said, is to study and examine "the essence of the natural world".

Sometimes why should we cite the famous views of the scholars, philosophers and distinguished figures of the East and West while dealing with the harmony of religion, science and philosophy?

The status that a person is born with is an essential status, neither all-dimensional nor permanent an accidental status which has been gradually nurtured. The birth status, upbringing and primary training of man cannot imprison and deprive him of the capability to grow and advance to worldwide prominence. Great figures, like other individuals, belong to a specific place. Yet, their degree of personal excellence is such that they can duly be called "citizens of the world". Do the Westerners not say that Plato alone is history? Do the Easterners not say that Khwᵢjah Na¥īr al-Dīn al-±ūsī is "the teacher of humanity and the eleventh intellect" (mu'allim al-bashar wa 'l-'aql al-hᵢdī 'ashar)? Yes, they really mean what they say. Therefore, quoting the views of prominent and pioneering figures of religion, philosophy and science in every region is actually quoting the views of a person who is the son of humanity and whose homeland is the world.

First reason: Sometimes, citing the views of prominent figures proves that the issue in question is so important that it has drawn the attention of those figures, because it is correct and constructive work.

Second reason: There are also times when citing the views of others substantiates the reply that comes to the mind of a thinker.

In other words, it is for the sake of religion that the certainty of the said thinker might increase, or those who are interested in his view pay more attention to it.

Third reason: The laity is under the influence of the views of great and famous figures. Sometimes, this feeling is so strong that all the mental powers of those people are under their influence. It is at this juncture, that the scientific, philosophical, religious, and cultural authorities of society bear the heavy responsibility of preventing people to treat their figures' views as absolute. During the Middle Ages in the West and in some places in the East, if only the authorities had prevented the thinkers from going to extremes while appraising the philosophers of ancient Greece, human knowledge would have attained a higher and more profound level.

Fourth reason: In the course of history, the emergence of great civilizations has drawn the attention of nations that interact with the people of those civilizations; for example, the Mesopotamian Civilization, Byzantium Civilization, Islamic Civilization, and Westnern Civilization in recent times.

It is clear that the elements that constitute civilization are diverse; for example, economy, arts, science, philosophy, religion, morality, industry, politics, law, and culture in its general sense. Unfortunately, in appraising these elements, mankind has not been able to adopt the moderate and logical way as is supposed. In the same manner, it has always failed to find out the ultimate cause of the emergence, advancement, decline, and fall of civilizations.

For example, nowadays, the technological element of civilization in the West is highly praised and considered absolute and not only majorly reduced the advanced, constructive religion, morality and culture but also expelled social sciences from the scene! It is due to this technological advancement and progress that the West hold destructive supremacy over other cultures and civilizations in all scientific, philosophical, religious, and cultural issues. This undue supremacy has made their correct set of scientific, philosophical, religious, cultural, and moral subjects unquestionably credible for the common people, particularly the unsuspecting youth. Thus, the dedicated scholars consider themselves duty-bound to cite the acceptable views of outstanding figures in the technological advanced societies to draw the attention of such people and awaken their own society.

Fifth reason: To call the attention of those who are new in the arena of knowledge and learning to the important fact that if figures from technologically advanced countries have deviated from the established principles and values in society, there are other personalities, in the same countries, who believe in and live by those principles and values. Citing views with this purpose is something very useful and valuable.

The Views of Some Ancient Philosophers on the Essential Reality of Things

1. Plato's Theory of Ideas: Plato believes that supernatural and intelligible truths are the origin of the universe and that all the creatures we can perceive in the world and with which we interact, are shadows of those truths.[1] Both Plato and Kips agree that the parts that constitute the natural bodies are small and diverse.[2]

2. Thales' "Water as the Origin": From India, California and Mesopotamia up to Thales[3] who said, "Every physical transformation needs living elements."[4]

3. Samkhya:[5] A universal soul or a world originates from

---

1. Plato, Jumh£riyyat (Republic), trans. °ann¡ Khabb¡z, pp. 183-187 (originally in Greek).
2. Aristotle, Kawn wa Fas¡d (On the Generation and Corruption), Part 8, para. 9, p. 182, as quoted from Plato's Timaeus.
3. S¡m¢ 'Al¢ Nish¡r, Nish¡' al-D¢n, pp. 194-195.
Thales of Miletus (c. 640 – c. 546 B.C.): Greek philosopher and scientist; recognized as the founder of Greek philosophy or first who made name as a philosopher; one of the Seven Wise Men of Greece. [Trans.]
4. Mu!ammad Far¢d Wajd¢, Barkhar¡beh-h¡-ye M¡dd¢, p. 27.
5. Samkhya, also Sankhya, S¢mkhya, or S¢nkhya: one of the six schools of classical Indian philosophy. [Trans.]

spirits, which are limitless and peerless.[1]

4. Hindu concept of the unity of beings: Bashan is "the divine truth of which all creatures of the natural world are parts." (That is the Hindu concept of the unity of all beings and a number of philosophers prior to Socrates.)[2]

5. Anaximenes,[3] Diogenes Laertius[4] and Archelaus[5] regard air as the truth of beings.[6]

6. Heraclides:[7] "The fire (essential reality of the world of nature) and the Logos (the Intellect extended in the world) [constitute God]."[8]

7. Pythagoras[9] has mentioned a number and a single essence as the origin of all beings and numbers without defining it.[10]

8. Democritus:[11] "Truths are unobservable. Natural bodies consist of tiny particles." In defining these particles, Democritus has used the word "eidos" or "eidolon" which is used for

1. Dr. Muḥammad Ghilᵢb, Mushkilat al-UlⱠhiyyah, p. 165.
2. Ibid., p. 124.
3. Anaximenes of Miletus (585 – 528 BCE): an Archaic Greek Pre-Socratic philosopher active in the latter half of the 6th century BC. [Trans.]
4. Diogenes Laertius (c. 3rd century CE): a biographer of the Greek philosophers and whose surviving Lives and Opinions of Eminent Philosophers is one of the principal surviving sources for the history of Greek philosophy. [Trans.]
5. Archelaus (5th century BCE): an Ancient Greek philosopher and a pupil of Anaxagoras. [Trans.]
6. Oswald Kulpeh (?), Muqaddameh-ye Falsafeh (An Introduction to Philosophy), p. 165.
7. Heraclides Ponticus (c. 390 BC – c. 310 BC), also known as Herakleides and Heraklides of Pontus: a Greek philosopher and astronomer who lived and died at Heraclea Pontica, now Karadeniz Ereğli, Turkey. [Trans.]
8. YⱠsuf Karam, TᵢrⱠkh-e Falsafeh-ye YⱠnᵢnⱠ, p. 87; 'Abd al-Raḥmᵢn BadawⱠ, KharⱠf al-Fikr al-YⱠnᵢnⱠ, p. 87.
9. Pythagoras of Samos (c. 672-497 B.C.): the founder of Pythagoreanism, a philosophical, mathematical, moral and religious school, one of whose basic principles was that the substance of things is 'number' and that all phenomena can be understood in mathematical ratios. [Trans.]
10. Aristotle, Mᵢ Ba'd al-±abᵢ'ah (Metaphysics), part 5.
11. Democritus of Abdera (c. 460-370 B.C.): famous in Muslim philosophy for his theory of atoms; generally considered to be the founder of Greek atomism and also of the notion of empty space. [Trans.]

abstract truths.[1]

9. Anaxagoras[2] has brought forth four things: (1) air,[3] (2) dust,[4] (3) primary matter,[5] and (4) various elements.[6]

10. Stoicism:[7] The Stoics regard matter as the perfect abode or life.[8] Physically, the Stoics believe that Nature has been created from two origins: the active and passive substances.[9]

11. Parmenides:[10]

The Intelligent One is the origin and truth of all beings.[11]

12. Euclides of Megara[12] agrees with Parmenides that the essence of things is an indivisible one.[13]

13. St. Bonaventure:[14] St. Bonaventure agrees with the Augustinians that creatures are composed of essence and being, primary matter and form… and that the primary matter has the primary particles.[15]

14. Empedocles:[16] He believed that water and fire, earth and

---

1. Ri¤¡ Tawf¢q, Q¡m£s-e Falsafeh (Philosophical Dictionary) under "Democritus".

2. Anaxagoras (c. 500 BC – 428 BC): a Pre-Socratic Greek philosopher. [Trans.]

3. Aristotle, Kit¡b-e Nafs, p. 14.

4. Oswald Kulpeh, Madkhal-e Falsafeh, p. 156.

5. Ibid.

6. Aristotle, Kawn wa Fas¡d (On the Generation and Corruption), p. 108.

7. Stoicism: a school of Hellenistic philosophy founded in Athens by Zeno of Citium in the early 3rd century BC, and maintains that destructive emotions resulted from errors in judgment. [Trans.]

8. 'Abd al-Ra¦m¡n Badaw¢, Khar¢f al-Fikr al-Yun¡n¢, pp. 27-28.

9. Andre Carlson, M¡rk Awril¥£s – Fal¡sefeh-ye Buzurg (Marcus Aurelius – The Great Philosophers), trans. K¡¨im 'Im¡d¢.

10. Parmenides of Elea (fl. early 5th century BCE): an ancient Greek philosopher who was the founder of the Eleatic school of philosophy. [Trans.]

11. Al-Ta¦q¢q f¢ M¢l¢sy£s wa Iks¢n£f¢n wa Gharghy¢s, p. 274 (as quoted from Aristotle, Kawn wa Fis¢d (On the Generation and Corruption).

12. Euclides of Megara (450 ? – 374 BCE): Greek Eleatic philosopher, contemporary of Plato, and like him, disciple of Socrates; founder of the Megarian school. [Trans.]

13. Qissat al-Falsafat al-Y£n¡niyyah, p. 136.

14. St. Bonaventure (1221 – 1274), born John of Fidanza: an Italian medieval scholastic theologian and philosopher. [Trans.]

15. Dr. Y£suf Karam, T¡r¢kh al-Falsafat al-Ur£biyyah f¢ 'l-'A¥r al-Wasa§ (The History of European Philosophy in the Middle Ages), p. 47.

16. Empedocles, known to Muslim philosophers by other Arabic variants of his

wind, love and hatred were forces of attraction and repulsion.[1] The other recorded view of Empedocles is that the primary substance of things is ether, which cannot be corrupted and it is assumed that all realities are created from small particles of countless ether.[2]

15. Neoplatonism:[3]

The Truth of the universe is living.[4]

16. Zeno of Elea:[5]

The essence of the Real Being is still and motionless.[6]

17. Marcus Aurelius Antoninus:[7]

The brightness of the sun does not have more than one existence although it is indefinitely dispersed and shines over walls, mountains and other places." And it is only one entity although it is dispersed in an indefinite number of specific natures and bodies. "And an Intelligent Spirit does not have more than one being notwithstanding outward divisions. Intelligent beings always benefit from this single and exclusive Intelligent and each of them is mutually related because of this benefit ...[8]

---

name: Abidqulis, Abidhqulis, etc. (c. 490 – c. 435 BCE): a pre-Socratic philosopher, physicist, physician and social reformer, who postulated the existence of the four elements or roots out of the mixture of which all things came to be, love and hate being the cause of motion and so of the mixing of these elements. [Trans.]

1. Aristotle, Kitịb-e Nafs, p. 16.

2. Khwịjah Naᶍᶜr al-Dᶜn al-ᵗ£sᶜ, Muqaddimah Bᶜ' al-Nafs Bad Fanᵢ' al-ᵒabsah.

3. Neoplatonism: the modern term for a school of religious and mystical philosophy that took shape in the 3rd century CE, based on the teachings of Plato and earlier Platonists, with its earliest contributor believed to be Plotinus, and his teacher Ammonius Saccas. [Trans.]

4. Dr. Muᵎammad Ghulịb, Mushkilat al-Ul£hiyyah, p. 125 (as quoted from the book £pᶜnᶜshᶜd-e Brahman, p. 274).

5. Zeno of Elea (490 – 430 BCE): a Greek philosopher and student-defender of Parmenides, who is known for his paradoxes of space, time, motion and change. [Trans.]

6. Aᵎmad Amᶜn Zakᶜ Najᶜb Maᵎmᶜd, Qiᶍᶍat al-Falsafah al-Y£nᵢniyyah, p. 45.

7. Marcus Aurelius Antoninus (121 – 180 CE): Roman Emperor from 161 to 180 (being the last of the "Five Good Emperors") and considered one of the most important Stoic philosophers. [Trans.]

8. Marcus Aurelius, Falᵢsᶜfeh ye Buᵣurg, p. 49.

Muslim philosophers and scholars;

(18) °usayn ibn 'Abd All¡h ibn Sīn¡ (Avicenna),

(19) Mu ! ammad ibn ±urkh¡n F¡r¡bī,

(20) Bahmany¡r,[1]

(21) Mu ! ammad ibn Zakariyy¡ R¡zī,[2]

(22) Īr¡nshahrī,[3]

(23) ¯adr al-Muta'allihīn Shīr¡zī,

(24) Mīr D¡m¡d,

(25) Khw¡jah Na¥īr al-Dīn al-±ūsī, and

(26) Mīr Findiriskī[4]: They all believe that the reality of things is unknown and what can be sought is the logical portion of things, or "to the extent of human comprehension" (*bi-qadr al-t¡'qat al-bashariyyah*). They say philosophy is the knowledge of the truths about creatures to the extent comprehensible to human beings.

27. According to Prof. Mu ! ammad Abdus Salam[5], the unity of forces invoked proves that this Single Power is yet to be physically defined.

28. Johannes Scotus Eriugena:[6]

All manifestations of existence of the objects and form are like forms in their primary essence.[7]

---

1. Ab£ 'l-°asan Bahmany¡r ibn Marzub¡n 'Ajam¢ ¡zerb¡yj¡n¢, known as Bahmany¡r (died 1067): a famous pupil of Avicenna, and of a Persian Zoroastrian background. [Trans.]

2. Mu ! ammad ibn Zakariyy¡ al-R¡z¢: the great Persian physician and chemist who discovered alcohol and authored a popular book in medicine entitled Al-°¡w¢. [Trans.]

3. Ab£ 'l-'Abb¡s ¡r¡nshahr¢: a 9th-century Persian philosopher, mathematician, natural scientist, historian of religion, astronomer, and author. [Trans.]

4. Sayyid M¢r Ab£ 'l-Q¡sim Astar¡b¡d¢, known as M¢r Findirisk¢ (1562 – 1640): a teacher of Mull¡ ¯adr¡ and a renowned Iranian philosopher, poet and mystic of the Safavid era. [Trans.]

5 The renowned Pakistani Nobelist physicist (Ed.)

6. Johannes Scotus Eriugena (c. 815 – c. 877 CE): an Irish theologian, Neoplatonist philosopher, and poet, known for having translated and made commentaries upon the work of Pseudo-Dionysius (a Christian theologian and philosopher of the late 5th to early 6th century). [Trans.]

7. Qi¥¥at al-Falsafat al-°ad¢thah (originally in Arabic).

29. Meister Eckhart:[1]

The universe we have access to, that is, the world of creatures and material things, is a model and prototype of the Universal Reason.[2]

30. Jalįl al-Dīn Muḥammad Mawlawī (Rūmī):

The whole world is the form of Universal Reason, which is the father of whosoever is a follower of the Word.[3]

31. Giordano Bruno:[4] Bruno adds this point to the theory of Democritus about indivisible particles:

Ether is a fluid that fills the air, and the tiny particles of this fluid substance called 'monads' are indivisible impenetrable units of substance, and it is the same units of substances that bring about interaction, cause and effect of different materials and forms.[5]

The entire world of being is living, and there is a Universal Spirit in all realities of the permanent beings, and no part of the universe at all is lifeless. Without doubt, these beings are an integral part of a Source of activity from which the different kinds of creatures originate, just as the rays of the sun originate from the sun.[6]

32. [Gottfried Wilhelm] Leibniz:

We know that each of the utilitarian dimensions, mechanisms and metaphysical realities of the creatures is correct in its own right. The mechanism in the outward and apparent dimension as well as the 'monads' in the inward dimension are pure.[7]

---

1. Eckhart von Hochheim O.P., commonly known as Meister Eckhart (c. 1260 – c. 1327): a German theologian, philosopher, and mystic. [Trans.]
2. S.S. Frost (?), U¥£l-e Ta'lçm-e Falįsefeh-ye Buzurg (Principles of the Teachings of Great Philosophers), p. 30. [Trans.]
3. Rumi's *Masnavi*, Book 4, line 3259, p. 365. [Trans.]
4. Giordano Bruno, born Filippo Bruno (1548 – 1600): an Italian Dominican friar, philosopher, mathematician and astronomer. [Trans.]
5. Qi¥¥at al-Falsafat al-°adçthah, p. 43.
6. Ibid., p. 44; Tįrₑkh al-Falsafat al-°adçthah, pp. 34-36.
7. Ibid., p. 124.

The explanation of this meaning is that every individual essence (monad) is a universe in itself; that is, that which exists in all essences of the universe is present in every essence and each of the essences is the reflection of the whole visage of the entire universe. It is as if the entire universe is reflected in it except that every essence potentially encompasses a certain degree of the truth and another degree actually.

The degree in which the truth is actually reflected in it pertains to its perception, and the degree in every individual differs according to the intangible differences. The root of essence is interlinked or attached to one another... and, it can also be said that a perspective through which the universe can be seen, except that the extent of the perspectives differs with one another—some wide, while others narrow.

33. Herbert:

> *Contradictory meaning, especially in philosophy, pertains to matter, time, place, movement, essence, accident, and cause. But since matter and time are both multiplicable, they are common because they are divisible, and it is the principle of contradictions which exists in the drinking-place of Zeno and Kant. Movement is the fusion of being and non-being. Quiddity (jawhar) means just a single thing which is divisible on account of accidents and powers, while cause—if it is external—means that a being is affected by a causality which was in the past, and not [on account of being impressed or changed]. If it has been changed without taking any consideration, it is the same previous state, and if it were an internal cause such as a volitional action, then it signifies the agency, and being the object of action of the single thing.*

To takle the seeming contradiction, one needs to say that what exists externally is not only that which has been tangible for us from the beginning, and multiplying. They are rather qualities contrary to the tangible ones and each of them is simple and absolute in its own right, and all things perceivable by our senses are a compound we have made. Therefore, they are both essential and relative at the same time and have no contradiction in the absoluteness of the qualities because our beings, like Leibniz's monads, are protracted, with the only difference that our beings consist of different states. In fact, they are simple (bas¡yit) at the peak of simpleness (bas¡tat) and lack change; they are permanently stable and the changes that take place are only in the variant attachments of the qualities and not in their essence. It is in this way that Herbert resolves contradiction.[1]

34. Fichte:[2]

> Since what the people regard as 'existence' —whether accidents or essences —have no reality and are [mere] forms, there is no 'was' and [only] 'is' exists, and that which has reality is the same 'I'. (Here, we also refrain from using the term 'self' or 'mind' for it may give us a wrong impression). The acquisition of knowledge is such that initially the 'I' comes to its senses, becomes aware of itself or finds itself out. At this point, Fichte uses an expression which we may suggest 'to make up' (wax'). In this case, in the words of Fichte it can be said thus, "The 'I' makes up itself" or establishes its essence, but I think if we use the Persian equivalent of wax' which is 'to mold' (bar nih¡dan), it would be more compatible with Fichte's expression. Hence, he says, "First, the 'I' molds itself." In essence, the 'I' is unlimited but since it molds itself, giving it distinction and confidence, it [actually] limits itself because to be distinguished and determined implies being limited, and the unlimited cannot be distinguished and determined. The very act of the 'I' limiting itself [is] 'other than I'; that is, the tangible world or that which is called the world outside the mind will be realized. In other words, the existence of 'other than I', that is, the things —big and small—and the entire external world is [possible] through the limit which corresponds to the 'I' and strikes at the 'other than I'. That is to say, it makes divisible that which is indivisible. It

---

1. T¡rɛkh al-Falsafat al-°adɛthah, p. 270 (originally in Arabic).
2. Johann Gottlieb Fichte (1762 – 1814): a German philosopher and a founding figure of the philosophical movement known as German idealism, a movement that developed from the theoretical and ethical writings of Immanuel Kant. [Trans.]

thus becomes clear that the 'other than I' is a creation of the 'I'. The 'I' is the subject while the 'other than I' is an object. The 'I' is the knower while the 'other than I' is the unknowing object to be known. In this manner, it becomes clear that the knower and the known is one and the same, and the 'other than I' is nothing. We know that the 'I' is not completely defined in the philosophy of Fichte. It only clarifies the point that the essence of things is something extra natural.[1]

35. Schelling:[2] The main difference between the philosophy of Fichte and that of Schelling lies in the fact that Fichte regards the phenomenal or objective world as unreal, limiting truth to the noumenal and subjective realm, while Schelling believes in the world as real. However, Schelling supposes that the world and the 'I' are either objective or subjective; that is, the souls are of one type and of one origin, and each one of them is not absolute truth, or the creator, or created by another. The same power, which exists in the soul or spirit, also exists in nature. Each of them subsists, parallel with the other, in following the same rule, and it is in this way that we can realize the existence of nature and understand how the soul is nourished in the world. In reality, the world of nature undergoes the same process of the soul for its nourishment. Thus, there must be another Power in nature, which is different from the outward power, which is tangible. In other words, according to Fichte, there is something in the soul, which is opposed by a restraining power through which whatever is within and outside the soul, is reconciled. This opposition must exist in nature as a whole, except that these opposing powers are weaker in nature in the sense that the "spiritual substance" is static and inert while the "material soul" which is activated is capacious."[3]

---

1. Muḥammad 'Alī Furūghī, Sayr-e ḥikmat dar Urūpī, vol. 2, pp. 11-12 (originally in Persian).

2. Friedrich Wilhelm Joseph Schelling, later von Schelling (1775 – 1854): a German philosopher who stands midpoint between his former mentor Fichte and former roommate Hegel in the development of German idealism. [Trans.]

3. Qiṣṣat al-Falsafat al-Ḥadīthah and Tārīkh al-Falsafat al-Ḥadīthah (both

36. George Wilhelm Friedrich Hegel:[1]

Being is of two types: (1) being by the senses which is particular and personal, and (2) being by the intellect which is universal or general." The tangible existent is proved to be devoid of reality and that which is real is the intelligible existent, and these two types of existents must not be separated from the philosophy of Hegel. When he says that a thing or a person who is "particular" has no reality and that reality is intelligible and universal, he does not mean that every "particular" has no external existence and every "universal" has external existence. It rather suggests that external existence means intelligible and useful to the time and space (because once it is not useful to the time and space, it cannot be discerned by the sensory perceptions). Its existence is not original, independent and intrinsic; it is rather accidental, and depends on the existence of the intellect and is a branch of it. The existence which is independent, genuine and intrinsic is intelligible, and this ruling is clarified in the statements of the philosophers who have founded critical philosophy. And we know that the existence of every existent depends on the conception or knowledge about it in our minds. That is, the existence of all existents is secondary, relative and supplementary, with the exception of the intelligibles and conceptions whose existence does not depend on another thing, and if they are relative, this is only in relation to themselves; hence, they are original, independent and intrinsic..." And this is one of the famous statements of Hegel: "That which is real and realized is intelligible and that which is intelligible is realized because it is obvious that that which is real cannot be contrary to the intellect and that which is affirmed by the intellect cannot be unreal.[2]

What is relevant of Hegel's theory in respect of our debate is

---

originally in Arabic).

1. Georg Wilhelm Friedrich Hegel (1770-1831): a German philosopher, one of the creators of German idealism, and along with Immanuel Kant, one of the most influential philosophers of the Age of Enlightenment. [Trans.]

2. Sayr-e ʿikmat dar Uɪ£pi, vol. 3, p. 64.

that since the concrete existents are secondary, depend on the intellect, and attached to the more comprehensive "I", it is impossible to know them except through the intellect.

37. Felicite Robert de Lamennais:[1]

The reason of the atheist in denying the Real Origin is His [alleged] weakness and impotence and the incompatability of such a 'god' with the natural and creative evils. Given this description, however, this materialist has acquired faith in certain matters, which he has never understood; for example, gravitation, locomotion, matter, and mind. What a folly! If a materialist could have defined a grain of sand to me, I could have explained God to him.[2]

It is the gradual manifestation of the Real Essence in time and space which leads toward perfection but will never reach perfection because if it is perfect then it will never be created. The stages of perfection begin with the inanimate objects and proceed to the living creatures, and in the lower stages, in which materiality prevails; the world is the world of constraint no matter how one progresses, and the world becomes the world of compulsion.[3]

38. Jean-Marie Guyau:[4]

This young scholar regards the origin or truth of all existents as living.[5]

The gist of Guyau's view is that the origin or truth in the world is indeed life and life is diverse throughout the world. That is, it is life, which is yet to flourish, or life, which extends.

However, the truth about life must be seen. According to Guyau, the truth of life is enhancement, expansion, empowerment, and spreading out. But, it is enhancement of the

1 Hugues-Félicité Robert de Lamennais (1782-1854), was a French Catholic priest, philosopher, and political theorist. He was one of the most influential intellectuals of Restoration France (Ed.)

2. Ibid.

3. Ibid.

4. Jean-Marie Guyau (1854 – 1888): a French philosopher and poet. [Trans.]

5. Sayr-e °ikmat dar Ur£p¡, vol. 3, p. 143.

self and not taking something from others and adding it to oneself, or spreading out to despise others; it is rather innovation and self-bestowal. It is in the nature of life to be enhanced as well as to extend. Its enhancement means to make use of and show its power and talent. Its expansion means that its powers, including mental power, skills, feelings, or determination, must go beyond itself and reach others.

[Since Guyau's moral philosophy is about a highly exalted life, we shall also quote his pertinent statements here:] "Complete life is to make use of it for others. Absolute selfishness is incompatible with life; it is mere desiring for, limiting and reducing oneself. If there were no existence and grace, there would be death, because life will not last long unless it is spread out. This is the pinnacle of selfishness in the zenith of selflessness, and morality cannot be individualistic; in fact, by necessity, it must be collective. If a person does not live in a group, then what is the meaning of life [for him]? If existence is not coupled with enhancement, bestowal and grace, how can it be called "life" and if it is not so, how can grace be expressed? Therefore, sense of morality, i.e. selflessness, is not based upon right and duty because it is a necessity of life, and this is the truth. It is also for this reason that it earns no reward because to be good is harmonious with nature while to be wicked is repugnant to it. Even in a collectivity, if acting against the sense of morality incurs punishment, it is not for revenge and retaliation. It is rather for the sake of protection and preservation of society. Forgiving and compassion are not traits of the lower class but part of the disposition and nature of the nobles." Guyau also said, "I hold the hands of my companions with my one hand and my other hand is meant to hold the hands of the weak. In fact, I don't mind extending both my hands to the weak.

39. Hermann Lotze:[1] Lotze objected to the Romantic philosophers for not taking into consideration the phenomenon of nature and criticized the materialist philosophers for taking

---

1. Rudolf Hermann Lotze (1817 – 1881): a German philosopher and logician. [Trans.]

into account the form and layer of existence, and he himself believes that each of the two aspects of existence must be reflected upon. There is no doubt that the world has spiritual and intelligible reality which everyone must realize, but one can seek the inward aspect in the outward affairs and the soul can be found in the body. With respect to the world of natural affairs, Lotze's view can be summed up as follows: We can find the things in the world to be multiple but we can see that they interact with each other. As such, we can find out that those things are not independent of each other because an independent person's influence upon another person has no meaning. Thus, things are not independent and separate from each other and they have an intangible relationship with each other. In other words, what we can see are different states of One Original Existent that encompasses everything and from which everything originates. [Concerning] the belief of naturalists on the essence of existents, which have integral parts, Lotze synthesizes and adapts the belief of Leibniz .He believes in the existent, with integral parts, as a central force having no dimensions, for dimension, like other tangible qualities, is a product of interaction between and among the integral parts. That is to say, the integral parts are not corporeal; they are states in which the original, real and infinite existent takes form.

40. Herbert Spencer:

> Take science serious. May it convince you and answers all questions of the intellect. Ask science, 'What is the essence of this tangible matter which has filled space?' Science will reply, 'If you cut it apart, you will find out its smaller parts.' Then, you will ask science again, 'Can these parts be cut apart infinitely or will it reach a point when these parts can no longer be divisible?' Both aspects of the issue must be shunned and without formulating a solution for itself, the intellect will surprisingly come to a standstill. After this question, ask the intellect again, 'What is the faculty [of senses]?' We do not think science can

convince you with a correct answer.[1]

41. Alfred Jules Émile Fouillée[2]: "Alfred Fouillée was one of the spirtualist philosophers. He regarded the intelligible, [conceivable or ideational] matter as the truth and in this regard, his way of thinking was not new... Apart from recognizing all realities of the world as intelligible and emanating from the Intelligent, Alfred Fauvi treats knowledge and willpower in man's being as a single faculty in contrast to most philosophers who make a distinction between them and treat them as two faculties."[3]

42. Hermann von Helmholtz: "In this work, whose title is about the perpetuity of force, he has conducted a general study of the issue of thermodynamics. He has stated:

> *Since work, heat and electricity cannot be converted into one another, it is clear that they are various specific forms. That which is specific is not susceptible to change and sometimes we observe it as heat; at times, as light. Once it is in the form of mechanical work, we can observe chemical and electrical energy, and this refers to 'energy'. The entire world of nature stems from large and inalterable amounts of energy which appear to us in various forms, and now they are together in terms of quantity.*[4]

***

> *We must bear in mind that energy which is defined as "the primary substance of things" is purely theoretical from the perspective of physics. According to Max Planck, Helmholtz believes in supernatural realities while talking about the fundamental reality of the world of nature. Planck thus says, "The measurements of the physicists never teach him anything about the real world. For him, measurements are nothing but*

---

1. Herbert Spencer's "Mabjd¢-e [U¥£l-e] Nakhust¢n (The Origins of Primary Principles)," as quoted in Qi¥¥at al-Falsafat al-°ad¢thah, pp. 477, 778 (originally in Arabic).

2 Alfred Jules Émile Fouillée (1838-1912) was a French philosopher (Ed.)

3. Sayr-e °ikmat dar Ur£pj, vol. 3, p. 141.

4 Tjr¢kh-e 'Ulfm (History of Science), trans. °asan ¯affjr¢, p. 612.

messages, which are more or less uncertain. In the words of Helmholtz himself, they are nothing but signs through which he can communicate with the real world. Thereafter, he strives to attain a document proving the remnants of an unknown civilization, and tries to achieve results from these endeavors. If a linguist wants to yield result, he must accept the principle that the document under consideration must incorporate the pertinent meaning. In the same vein, the physicists must take this idea as fundamental that the real world follows laws which are beyond our understanding.[1]

43. Herbert Spencer:

So, it must be known that there is something which is unknown, and the more the people of knowledge become knowledgeable of knowable things, the more they become ignorant of that unknown entity, for known things are accidents of the unknown entity...[2]

44. Blaise Pascal:[3]

When this weak man wants to plunge into or be knowledgeable with the world of nature, he stands in astonishment between two infinities — infinity in greatness and infinity in smallness. If you observe the human being in comparison to the world of nature and boundless outerspace, he is so small that there is no relationship between him and nature. It is here where science must find its causes and effects. No matter how the human mind wants to know its components, system and laws [from] the beginning up to the end, it cannot do so except with a set of common pieces of knowledge which are in the human market.[4]

45. Immanuel Kant:

---

1. Max Planck, Ta¥w¢r-e Jahın dar F¢z¢k-e Jad¢d (The Image of the World in Modern Physics), trans. Murtaªı ¯ıbir, p. 138 (originally in English).

2. Sayr-e °ikmat dar Ur£pı, vol. 3, pp. 105-106.

3. Blaise Pascal (1623-1662): a French mathematician, physicist and religious philosopher. [Trans.]

4. Tır¢kh al-Falsafat al-°ad¢thah, p. 86.

I am neither a Sophist nor a Puritanist; neither do I negate creatures nor deny God; nor do I regard science and philosophy as meaningless. I have objections against the human intellect, appraising its standard and determining its limit, to make clear to what extent the intellect can reach and cannot reach, and I say that our intellects' understanding only perceives the outward and accidental aspects of the existents and can only discern the science dealing with natural things. That is, that which can be experimented and if they take fundamentals from us, intellection will have no more bearing for us.[1]

46. John Locke:[2]

Whether matter can think, or not? We have no way of solving this problem because we do not know and understand the truth of the essence of matter except through ideas, which we call 'essence'. Hence, essence is something unknown and what surround it are some traits which can be perceived by the senses.[3]

47. Maine de Biran:

A study of the essence of the soul as has been done by past philosophers is an exercise in futility because the essence cannot be understood.[4]

48. Auguste Comte:

...The second school of truth for things, establishes the transcendence of phenomena but he regards it impossible to identify it. The forerunners of this Kantian school are Kant and Herbert Spencer.[5]

49. Bernard Bolzano:[6]

1. Sayr-e °ikmat dar Ur£p¡, vol. 2, p. 247.

2. John Locke (1632-1704): an English physician and philosopher. [Trans.]

3. T¡r¢kh al-Falsafat al-°ad¢thah, p. 221.

4. Sayr-e °ikmat dar Ur£p¡, vol. 3, p. 105.

5. Asas al-Falsafah, pp. 146-147.

6. Bernhard Placidus Johann Nepomuk Bolzano, Bernard Borzano in English (1781 – 1848): a Bohemian mathematician, logician, philosopher, theologian,

The mathematicians and Aristotelian logicians opposed pragmatism. They believed that among the realities and phenomena, there is an absolute truth which is totally independent and without any relationship with experiments and experimentations. Given its standing, this absolute [entity] cannot be limited by time, space and attributes. So, this is an absolute inalterable truth which, in all objectivity, is permanent and needless of the intellect to perceive its existence. Among those who subscribe to this school is Bernard Bolzano who explains that the truth will essentially remain with the same eternal permanence and independence.[1]

50. Voltaire:[2]

Since we cannot have any knowledge except through experiment, it is impossible for us to know what matter is. We can see and feel the properties of this essence but this very word 'essence', that is, that which is covered and hidden, tells us that this covered and hidden entity shall always be unknown and no matter how much we discover its external dimensions, still this concealed thing will always remain unknown to us.[3]

51. George Santayana:

I am sincere in materialist philosophy but I do not think I have understood the real meaning of matter and it is also necessary for the scholars to make me understand what matter really is. And I say that matter is exactly like mentioning the name of a close friend 'Sam Jones' without knowing him fully. In fact, we are only familiar with his outward personality.[4]

52. Regarding the interpretation and analysis of things

Catholic priest and antimilitarist of German mother tongue. [Trans.]

1. Ibid., p. 186.

2. François-Marie Arouet, better known by the pen name Voltaire (1694-1778): a French Enlightenment writer and philosopher famous for his wit and advocacy for civil liberties. [Trans.]

3. Andre Cresson, "Voltaire" in Falؚsefeh-ye Buzurg (The Great Philosophers).

4. Qiⱶⱶat al-Falsafat al-°adؚthah, p. 510.

through matter, Joseph de Meister has opposed modern philosophers, saying:

> *Matter has no causality at all ... And we do not know of anybody who can comprehend all realities and every level of existents as confined to or limited by a superior existent. Perhaps, there might be levels of superior existents which are beyond our comprehension.*[1]

53. Antoine Kernu:

> *It is natural for us to know the things in terms of [their] connection with us and not their absolute reality.*[2]

54. Oliver Lodge:

> *But we do not really know all laws governing this substance. In fact, we tread a path, which leads us to this knowledge. In this regard, the natural scientists hold diverse beliefs and assumptions which exceed hundreds, and since it is an ambiguous and unfathomable subject, it is beyond human comprehension.*[3]

55. Nicolas Malebranche:[4]

> *Man has no knowledge of the physical bodies but he can understand their mental images which exist in the beginning.*[5]

56. Schopenhauer:[6]

> *How can the materialists define the intellect by matter while we understand matter itself through the intellect?! ...It is impossible for us to understand the truth as long as we commence the discussion and study with matter, while this*

---

1. Tįrɛkh al-Falsafat al-°adɛthah, p. 294.

2. Ibid., pp. 256-257.

3. ¯ubhɛ, "'Aqį'id-e Oliver Lodge" in Falsafeh-ye Takwɛn (originally in Persian).

4. Nicolas Malebranche (1638 – 1715): a French Oratorian and rationalist philosopher. [Trans.]

5. Tįrɛkh al-Falsafat al-°adɛthah, p. 126.

6. Arthur Schopenhauer (1788 – 1860): a German philosopher known for his pessimism and philosophical clarity [Trans.]

tangible thing is a direct creation of ours.[1]

57. Jean Filo:

In order to define time, we must have complete and ultimate knowledge of physics. Fortunately, this branch of science always deals with measurements and not with definite concepts. Physical science limits itself to determining a series of transcendental approximations, provided that these approximations are close to one another.[2]

58. Baruch Spinoza:[3]

We know the essence of truth but through its attributes which, in turn, means what the intellect can comprehend and materialize is a quiddity. An infinite essence has infinite attributes and every attribute signifies constancy of an eternal quiddity, and we have no knowledge except that of the attributes; except thinking and spatium.[4]

59. William Hamilton:[5]

He is a follower of Kant and regards the human intellect as incapable of perceiving the absolute and only capable of perceiving relative things. And the power of the human intellect cannot discern anything except by limiting, restricting and laying a condition to it. In reality, human perception of a thing has no meaning except limiting and restricting it. Similarly, philosophy is nothing except limiting a thing… and we cannot have knowledge of anything except comparing it to ourselves or

---

1. Qi¥¥at al-Falsafat al-°ad¢thah, p. 402.

2. Jean T., F¡l£ °¡fi¨eh-Zam¡n.

3. Baruch de Spinoza, later Benedict de Spinoza (1632 – 1677): a Dutch rationalist philosopher. [Trans.]

4. T¡r¢kh al-Falsafat al-°ad¢thah, p. 107; 'Abd al-Ra¦m¡n Badaw¢, Rab¢' al-Fikr al-Y£n¡n¢, p. 125; Qi¥¥at al-Falsafat al-°ad¢thah, p. 15; "Spinoza," Falsafeh-ye Buzurg (The Great Philosophers).

5. Sir William Hamilton, 9th Baronet (1788 – 1856): a Scottish metaphysician. [Trans.]

something else which is known to us...[1]

60. Thomas Carlyle:[2]

But science portrays nature without knowing its meaning."[3]
"Yet, he also had a philosophical view in this regard, and was inclined towards German philosophers. He believed in a form and meaning for every thing just as the image of the human being is that of a four-footed animal that covers its body, but its meaning is spirit and divine entity...

61. Gustav Theodor Fechner:[4]

Fechner explicitly and completely believes in spiritual unity and all existents as having a soul. He regards a particular as an integral part of a single soul ...[5]

62. Paul Langevin:[6]

From the very beginning, he had realized the extraordinary importance of Einstein's discovery and always corroborated with him in developing the results. For example, he was able to completely clarify the issue of the unity of matter...[7]

63. Tommaso Campanella:[8]

In every existent, there is a power from eternity through which

---

1. Sayr-e °ikmat dar Ur£pj, vol. 3, p. 79.

2. Thomas Carlyle (1795 – 1881): a Scottish satirical writer, essayist, historian and teacher during the Victorian era. [Trans.]

3. Sayr-e °ikmat dar Ur£pj, vol. 3, p. 79.

4. Gustav Theodor Fechner (1801 – 1887): a German experimental psychologist who was an early pioneer in experimental psychology and the founder of psychophysics. [Trans.]

5. Tjr¢kh al-Falsafat al-°ad¢thah, p. 375; Sayr-e °ikmat dar Ur£pj, vol. 3, p. 122.

6. Paul Langevin (1872 – 1946): a prominent French physicist who developed Langevin dynamics and the Langevin equation. [Trans.]

7. Tar¢kh-e 'Ul£m (The History of Science), p. 781.

8. Tommaso Campanella, baptized Giovanni Domenico Campanella (1568 – 1639): an Italian philosopher, theologian, astrologer, and poet. [Trans.]

it can make its essence move.[1]

64. Heidegger:[2]

This world has come to an end and is restricted, and it is possible to be destroyed suddenly by a destructive system. According to Heidegger, the universal system's power is value-based and is directly metaphysical in nature.[3]

65. Henri Poincaré:[4]

The axioms of our science are neither sensory nor real proofs. They are rather conventional matters and selected in such a way that they are interpreted as sensory proofs, and since the laws of science are conventional, they do not teach us anything of the reality or truth, for they only make known the human way of action or behavior.[5]

66. Hippolyte Taine:[6]

One of his distinctive features is that in spite of his inclination to positivism, he did not totally discard basic philosophy, believing that one can go beyond the outward and accidental and reach the essences and truths. He was not as hopeless as other positivist philosophers are in this regard. He said, "I consider my horizon limited and I can only discern my mind and I cannot determine the mind of a fellow human being.[7]

67. Friedrich Schiller:[8]

---

1. T¡r¢kh al-Falsafat al-°ad¢thah, p. 38.

2. Martin Heidegger (1889-1976): an influential German philosopher Martin Heidegger known for his existential and phenomenological explorations of the "question of Being." [Trans.]

3. Frost, U¥£l Ta'¡l¢m Fal¡sifeh-ye Buzurg, p. 171 (originally in Persian).

4. Jules Henri Poincaré (1854 – 1912): a French mathematician, theoretical physicist, engineer, and a philosopher of science. [Trans.]

5. Irtib¡§-e Ins¡n-Jah¡n (The Relationship between Man and Universe), vol. 3, p. 13 (originally in Persian).

6. Hippolyte Adolphe Taine (1828 – 1893): a French critic and historian. [Trans.]

7. Sayr-e °ikmat dar Ur£p¡, vol. 3, p. 134.

8. Ferdinand Canning Scott Schiller (1864 - 1937): a German-British philosopher.

In view of the difference of our stances, our views on things are diverse. Of those things, we do not perceive everything that must be perceived. In fact, among their elements and roots, we select what are given attention (or what attract our attention), and the relationship we set among things is meant for the goals and outcomes we contemplate in seeking for them. We formulate our verifications of sets of things, calling them logic, geometry, computation, and the like. So, all these sciences are replete with human orientation [and are determined by us]...[1]

68. Davies:[2]

The philosophy of Davies is neo-Hegelian, for while not accepting the absolute one, he nevertheless affirms particulars in contrast. Attempting to reconcile them he says, 'On one hand, thinking necessitates the absolute because the basic function of thinking is to give judgment and judgment has no value except when a high-level subject is materialized in our thinking, such that it is devoid of any sort of question and doubt which every judgment may necessitate. Thus, it is not real except when there is a single "I" that guarantees all ideas...[3]

69. Whitehead:

The notion of mass is losing its unique preeminence as being the one final permanent quantity... Mass now becomes the name for a quantity of energy considered in relation to some of its dynamical effects.' To such a low state have the mighty fallen.[4]

70. Nietzsche:

[Trans.]

1. Tjrɛkh al-Falsafat al-°adɛthah, p. 409.

2. Most probably, it refers to John Eric Langdon-Davies (1897–1971), a British journalist and author of books on military, scientific, historical, and Spanish (including Catalan) subjects. [Trans.]

3. Ibid., pp. 402-403.

4. Will Durant, The Pleasures of Philosophy (New York: Simon and Schuster, 1953), p. 40. [Trans.]

Boscovich[1] and Copernicus[2] have hitherto been the greatest and most successful opponents of ocular evidence.[3]

71. John Dewey:

There is no wonder Dewey concludes that 'the notion of matter actually found in the practice of science has nothing in common with the matter of materialists.' Could anything be more mystical and anomalous than this announcement, by physicists, that 'matter,' in the sense of spatial substance, has ceased to exist? The electrons, we are told, have none of the properties of matter: they are not solid, nor liquid, nor gaseous.

72. Lord Bertrand Russell:

He imagines that the universe is created from a substantial matter, and by 'substantial matter' he means particles of the fusion of matter and intellect in which the properties of matter and intellect cannot be found."[4] The definition of matter, according to Russell, is like the definition given by an Irish fisherman to his fishnet; that is, some holes which are put together by threads!

73. Langdon-Davies says, "He should have only added this to the definition:

... And its threads are also cut into pieces and only their knots have remained![5]

---

1. Roger Joseph Boscovich (1711 – 1787): a theologian, physicist, astronomer, mathematician, philosopher, diplomat, poet, Jesuit, and a polymath from Croatia, who studied and lived in Italy and France, and famous for his atomic theory. [Trans.]

2. Nicolaus Copernicus (1473-1543): the first astronomer to formulate a comprehensive heliocentric cosmology, which rejected the geocentric Ptolemaic system. [Trans.]

3. Ibid.

4. C.E.M. Joad, Muqaddameh bar Falsafeh-ye Jad¢d (Introduction to Modern Philosophy), p. 42.

5. Langdon-Davies, Shigift-h¡-ye Dur£n-e Atom (Marvels inside the Atom), p. 75 (originally in English).

74. Emile Boutroux:[1]

All natural laws are anchored in the rule and necessity of the cause and effect relationship. In reality, all forms of its expression constitute a rule, but on one hand, it must be noted that this rule and those laws are expressed orally according to the dictates of our intellects. We undertake matters according to our will, i.e. our desires and needs, and it is not certain if these are consistent with the truth. In other words, since we look at the affairs of the world, we have no option but to strive to make them consistent with our intellects and souls. How can our intellects be compatible with the Universal Intellect, making correct judgments, and our desire and wish become identical with the truth? Of course, the human being has no option but to give judgment on [different] affairs according to the dictates of his reason and look at them by taking account of his demands, i.e, his needs. Yet, it is certain that our intellects are incapable of comprehending the truth, and our desires which are part of our totality are not supposed to undermine the truth …[2]

75. Henri Bergson:[3]

The pieces of knowledge acquired through intellection and appear in the form of sciences and crafts are truths but they are relative and supplementary; they are not absolute truths and essential knowledge, and it is meant for something we have stated (life and its organization through certain means, instruments, methods, and the like)… So, according to Bergson, philosophy (in its technical sense) deals with knowledge about the essence of things and perceiving the truths, but this is not through intellection as we have explained, for intellection is actually conception and affirmation which are not real perception. Real perception is such that the perceiver and the

---

1. Étienne Émile Marie Boutroux (1845 – 1921): an eminent 19th century French philosopher of science and religion, and an historian of philosophy. [Trans.]

2. Sayr-e °ikmat dar Ur£p¡, vol. 3, p. 157.

3. Henri-Louis Bergson (1859-1941): a major French philosopher and evolutionist. [Trans.]

perceived must be one (the union of the intelligent and the intelligible) and this state cannot be attained by means of conception and affirmation, but rather through the intellect, and another faculty which Bergson calls literally, "inward view" [which perhaps means "inward intuition"] or "self-view". Bergson regards perception of the truth as its outcome, calling it 'philosophy', and thinking that the way of attaining it is not through reasoning, argumentation and presenting of proof but rather the "inward view.[1]

76. In a lecture at the Moscow State University, Umov,[2] a Russian physicist and philosopher, has said:

Life inside the atom exposes to us some properties. Perhaps, it might be different in spite of losing physical substances and while exhausting others. Yet, this truth is again kept away from us, which is beyond guessing. It is true but we have found out that the physical function is only in the description of the outward forms and searching for the existing relations among them; that is, it is not mere searching for the laws. Through its conceptual and systematic method, physics gets us closer to the single reality. This reality is very far from the limits of perceivable things. Once again, however, we recognized greatness of the truth, which is impossible to attain. This evolutionary perception is more scientific thinking; that is, laying down the foundation of thinking whose sequence is incessant and whose existence is perpetual.

77. Oswald Külpe:[3]

---

1. Sayr-e °ikmat dar Ur£p¡, vol. 3, pp. 171-172; Prof. Dr. Sergei Vayulov (?) (President of the Academy of Science), F¢z¢k-e N£r (The Light of Physics), quoting from the lecture of Umov in a jubilee celebration of the University of Moscow, p. 23. In the same page of the book, it is said that the Leader of the 1917 Revolution was present in the lecture, discerning well the value of it.

2. Nikolay Alekseevich Umov (1846 – 1915): a Russian physicist and mathematician known for discovering the concept of Umov-Poynting vector and Umov effect. [Trans.]

3. Oswald Külpe (1862 – 1915): one of the structural psychologists of the late 19th

That the theories conforming to the atomic world, which only pertain to the phenomena, do not go beyond the limits of experiment and what is beyond it, we must also consider are not in need of any reasoning because the shortcoming of our knowledge about the external world is something undeniable. Thus, the critics, realists and skeptics, in turn, do not deny this point.[1]

78. Albert Einstein:

It is so astounding that the science of physics has revealed so little and limited the external world for us. Our knowledge has limited our faculties of perception not only through conventional expedient factors (particular orientation) but rather by virtue of 'choosing'.[2]

***

The goal of science has never been to prove the inalterable truths and establish the definite and eternal beliefs. Science endeavors to gradually get closer to the truth, and, little by little, open the closed doors of the secrets of nature for mankind; to tear apart the curtains of ambiguity, one after another; to get closer to the summit of knowledge of the 'possible', without claiming attainment of 'the perfect and ultimate wellbeing' in any stages of one's perfection.[3]

***

The simplest thing which we can see is covered by mystery. This is the cradle of all real sciences and arts of man. Anyone who does not know this and is not amazed and astonished by this great mystery is dead. He is an unlit candle. Witnessing this mystery is great and to have knowledge of it is love, although it

---

and early 20th century. [Trans.]

1. Oswald Külpe, Muqaddameh bar Falsafeh (An Introduction to Philosophy), p. 32.

2. Bertrand Russell, The Meaning of Einstein's Relativity and Its Philosophical Repercussion. (Originally in English).

3. Ibid.

is mixed with fear (sense of prevailing immensity), which all religions brought about. Knowledge about the existence of things, which we cannot fathom, is the manifestations and reflections of the real form of things and the first cause of the radiation of their essence, and it can only be reasonable and probable through the simplest form and the most primary perspective. This profound feeling or this great excitement brings about religion and religious feeling. It is in this sense... and only in this sense that I am a religious and devoted person.[1]

***

But there is a belief and third religion without any exception although none of them can be found to have an identical and pure form." I consider it the religious feeling of creation or 'existence'. It is very problematic for me to explain this feeling to a person who is totally bereft of it. It is especially so, given the fact that there is no more discussion here of God who is portrayed in different forms. In this religion, one senses the insignificance of human hope and goals as well as magnificence and glory, which manifest beyond matters and phenomena in nature and ideas. He imagines his own being as a kind of prison just as he wants to be free from the cage of his body and find out the entire being all at once as a single truth.[2]

***

In my opinion, it is the most important function of art and science to stimulate this feeling and keep it alive in those who deserve.[3]

79. Max Planck:

The utmost aspiration of the physicist is to know the external real world, all of whose components are tools for his exploration. That is, his measurements never teach anything about the very real world. For him, measurements are nothing but messages

1. Albert Einstein, The World that I See. (Originally in English).

2. Ibid.

3. Ibid.

which are more or less uncertain. Or, in the words of Helmholtz, they are nothing but signs which communicate the real world to him. Thereafter, in the same way that the linguist strives to read a document from the remnants of an unknown civilization, he endeavors to get some conclusions from them. If the linguist wants to arrive at a certain conclusion, he must accept as a principle that the document under examination is meaningful. In the same manner, the physicists must regard the idea that the real world follows certain laws, which are beyond our comprehension as foundation. It is even necessary for him to abandon the hope of finding out those laws in totality or even determining the nature of those laws by means of determining the subject from the very beginning. By believing in the existence of such laws, the physicist builds and focuses his attention on a system of concepts and propositions for himself. That is, he pursues a better image to the extent possible from the physical world in such a way that it is as if this image is the real world as much as possible and sends those messages to the physicist.[1]

Max Planck has also touched on this subject in his other book whose specifics are indicated below.[2]

In order to simplify this subject, let us consider the following statements about "freewill":

... In a nutshell, it must be stated that if willpower is considered from without, it is positive but if it considered from within, it is free. By paying attention to this point, the problem can be solved — a problem which is only caused by the amalgamation of two irreconcilable viewpoints. Therefore, we are engrossed with a false problem (freewill). Today, perhaps, saying it is still objectionable, but I have no doubt that as time goes on, all will

---

1. Max Planck, The Image of the World in Modern Physics, (Originally in English).

2. Max Planck, Where is Science Going? (Originally in English).

have no option but to acknowledge it.[1]

This is an explicit expression, for, in view of its natural existence, the notion of willpower in the natural levels of the mind, which are adjacent to the natural dimension of our existence, submits to the law of causation. However, given the profound level of our mind (the conceiver of activities of our inward phenomena) willpower has freedom. Hence, any thing, which comes into being in the arena of nature and man, desires the truth or more profound truths. In the book entitled Jabr wa Ikhtiyar (Predetermination and Freewill) (1975), I have put forth the said theory in the following manner without having information whatsoever about Max Planck's statements:

> *Is willpower free? Most people say, 'I was free in my willpower to do such and such thing.' They also say sometimes, 'I was free in my willpower not to do such and such thing.' Nevertheless, at times they also say, 'In my willpower I was compelled to do or not to do such and such a thing.' Such myopic perception can also be seen in some great ideas. For example, in voluntary actions, willpower is presented as free, and in emergency and compulsory actions, willpower is assumed to be deterministic. But it seems that this classification, is inaccurate because from the totality of considerations that can be done about willpower, we arrive at the conclusion that willpower, which means to desire or to wish, cannot be described with 'freedom'.[2] In simpler terms, we have no 'free' willpower because willpower is an inner activity which is a product of the activity of one of the instincts. If it remains in its natural state it is a reflection and a sort of reaction, and if it is under the supervision and control of the wholesome[3] "I," it is an effect which is produced at the natural*

---

1. Ta¥w¢r-e Jah¦n dan F¢z¢k-e Jad¢d, p. 194.

2. In the book Jabr wa Ikhtiyar (Predetermination and Freewill), what has actually been used is 'presentation' instead of 'description' but the term 'description' is more accurate for our present purpose.

3. The word 'wholesome' is not in the book but it seems appropriate to put it; hence, we insert it here.

level of the soul in compulsory form under the supervision and control of the "I".[1] In other terms, though originating from the instinct's activity, since 'I' has the supervision and control, willpower has no option but to appear to be free. This veneer of freedom does not stem from willpower itself but rather from the "I" which has the supervision and control. If we examine closely the point that willpower is gradually produced in the state of "supervision and control of the 'I'" and runs its course, we can correctly discern that willpower by itself has no freedom.[2]

As such, among the most important examples of tracing appearances and their working to the concealed truth in this very world are our inner appearances and activities, which come into being with the management of the "I". In these cases of the "I," the said things are organized and administered from the outward levels of the human inner being.

80. Bertrand Russell:

For instance, we are similar to an inborn blind person who has been brought up by some great musicians, and through the relations existing among the musical notes and how to play them, he has learned the pertinent rules and he can read the musical notes and guide an orchestra. Now, if this inborn blind person can understand the explanations of others by means of signs and hints, little by little, he will become aware that musical notes, the movements of fingertips and other movements are representations of certain things completely different from the outward dimensions shown to him, but it is impossible for him to perceive their vocal representations. Now, our knowledge about nature is also something similar to it. We can read the 'notes' of nature and identify their written representations, but our inference of what things are represented by these notes is not

---

1. The exact text in the book Jabr wa Ikhtiyịr is "… which is produced by forced out of the supervision and control of the 'I' but the correct line is this: "…it is an effect which is produced in the natural level of the soul in compulsory form of the supervision and control of the 'I'."

2. M. T. Jafari, Predetermination and Freewill, pp. 82-83 (Originally in Persian).

more than the inference of a person on musical notes which represent certain things other than their apparent forms. The inborn blind person is superior to us in the sense that we are even deprived of living among people who hear the music of nature, and in reality, all of us are blind with respect to perceiving the notes of nature. There is no teacher beside us to hear the real tune of nature's notes and at least to guide us by hints and signs so as to perceive their essential qualities.[1]

If Russell and other thinkers of his intellectual bent—from the East and West—would have classified music into three: (1) physical sound with melody, and (2) spiritual sound with intuitive potential, the extremely instructive lessons of teachers would have been comprehensible and perceivable to us:

All particles, in movement at rest, are speakers:

Truly, to Him we are returning.

The praises and glorifications of the hidden particles have filled Heaven with an uproar.[2]

***

All particles on the earth and the heaven say to you during the day and night:

(They all say), "We have hearing and sight and are happy, (although) with you, the uninitiated, we are mute."[3]

(3) Sound behind the curtain of nature: It is impossible that the voices of the Prophets, Divine leaders and their successors would have been so sincere without hearing the behind-the-curtain voice of nature and thus influence the advancement of righteous civilizations, mold upright human beings and realize lofty human values.

Bertrand Russell says:

A truer image of the world, I think, is obtained by picturing

---

1. Bertrand Russell, The Meaning of Einstein's Relativity and Its Philosophical Repercussion.

2. Rumi's *Masnavi*, Book 3, lines 464-465, p. 53. [Trans.]

3. Ibid., Book 3, line 1019, p. 113. [Trans.]

things as entering into the stream of time from an eternal world outside, than from a view which regards time as the devouring tyrant of all that is. But in thought and in feeling, even though time be real, to realize the unimportance of time is the gate of wisdom.[1]

81. Bernard d'Espagnat:[2] "'Veiled realities' (Daspania's theory) holds that there is a non-physical reality independent from us which is beyond the framework of time and space and cannot be described with our current concepts. This independent reality has a cover on its face and one cannot describe it as it really is. This does not mean, however, that we cannot have access to it at all. The empirical reality of the physical world and the senses are two complementary reflections of this reality, and cannot be reduced into the physical concepts:

We have come to the conclusion that it (reality) cannot be known in full... Yet, can it be said that it cannot be known at all? Instead, I say that this reality has a cover on its face.[3]

***

D'Espagnat regards the explanation for phenomena as the last frontier of physics but at the same time, he believes that studying them shows us something of reality:

Firstly, I consider the viewpoint of realism to be correct and even inevitable and meaningfully current. At the same time, I know—this time from contemporary physics..., which does not confine the reality into that which can be described, that is, phenomena... By putting them together, it seems that I know that there is something beyond the phenomena. This, in my opinion, is real knowledge and it is very important.

Secondly, I believe that the primary laws of physics, in spite of

---

1. Bertrand Russell, Mysticism and Logic, p. 27.

2. Bernard d'Espagnat (b. 1921): a French theoretical physicist, philosopher of science, and best known author for his work on the nature of reality. [Trans.]

3. Mahdi Gulshani, An Analysis of the Philosophical Viewpoints of Contemporary Physicists, pp. 203-204 (Originally in Persian).

being unable to describe the reality as it really is, can acquire something from the reality with the existence of this human perspective, thus encompassing something indescribable from its structure. For me, this reasoning is very important to reasonably oppose the irreducibility of science, for I argue that if physics cannot acquire a perfect and certain description of the reality and yet encompass it, then why other ways such as music, painting and poetry cannot [have such a role]?[1]

***

D'Espagnat emphasizes that we must not confuse the empirical reality with the independent reality, stressing that other fields of knowledge can also show certain forms of the independent reality:

That which I call 'empirical reality' is the same set of phenomena... In my view, it is with this empirical reality that the ideas like 'complimentary' can be applied and it is the subject of rational knowledge known as 'science'. But this must not be confused with the independent reality; something whose complete description probably goes beyond the power of human intellect... Now, it seems rational [for us to accept] that other ways apart from science... can also provide along science something indescribable from the structure of independent reality.[2]

***

The ultimate wisdom that physics can teach us is that our perspective must at the same time focus on two levels which represent two meanings that philosophers call 'reality'. On one hand, we must think about independent reality... We must appreciate the source of phenomena, beauties and values and wish to be united with It. Meanwhile, we must know that this reality is like the unreachable horizon. On the other hand, we must not also be negligent in giving attention to the level of

---

1. Ibid.

2. Ibid.

empirical reality… The level of empirical reality is related to the things in life, perfection and even the world. We must give it its real importance… Without treating it identical with the ultimate horizon, it is something which shows the perfect subtlety of this wisdom.[1]

***

According to D'Espagnat, the difference between the veiled reality and the Kantian noumenon[2] is that we can acquire information about this veiled reality with the help of empirical means, for our theories are models, which acquire the approximation of the veiled reality without being able to describe it. There is a covering between the known and the unknown parts of reality, and the function of science is to expand the first realm and limit the second realm. [3]

***

As Einstein argues, "All are in unison that science must establish the relationship between and among the empirical truths, so that, based on the experimented truths, we can envisage other truths. According to the viewpoint of many positivists, obtaining the perfect answer to this investigation is the sole objective of science. However, I do not believe that such a particular objective causes the enthusiasm of the researcher that leads to great successes. There is a stronger, yet most ambiguous, motive after the untiring efforts that led to these successes. We want to discern the existence of reality. The foundation of all these efforts is the conviction, whose structural existence is perfectly coherent. Compared to the past, today we have lesser ground to allow ourselves to deviate from this

---

1. Ibid., p. 205.

2. Noumenon: a posited object or event that is known (if at all) without the use of the senses in contrast with, or in relation to "phenomenon," which refers to anything that appears to, or is an object of, the senses. [Trans.]

3. Mahdi Golshani, An Analysis of the Philosophical Viewpoints of Contemporary Physicists), p. 205.

astounding conviction.

Why we do not want to accept that probably new ways of describing reality is necessary, and that we have not yet succeeded in discovering them does not mean that it is the end of the road." [1]

82. Erwin Schrüdinger: [2]

Modern science is as far as the science of ancient Greeks in discovering the laws of nature. [3]

83. Werner Heisenberg – Mathematical forms:

Of course, in the field of atomic physics, many of the common old fields of physics will cease to exist; not only the applicability of their concepts and laws but even the whole concept of the reality... What the term 'reality' means is that there exist concrete phenomena regardless of whether they can be observed or not. One can no longer actualize these observations in atomic physics in this simple way. Here, we arrive at the conclusion that natural science does not deal with nature per se; it rather deals with nature the way man describes and understands it... This peculiarity of the quantum theory makes it a problem for us to accept the system acceptable to the philosophy of materialism and to regard the smallest particles of matter, i.e. the basic particles, as existing in the true sense of the word. This is because if the quantum theory is correct, these basic particles are not real as in the case of usual things such as tree and stone. In fact, it seems that it is the abstractions of the observations, which have reality. If it is impossible to attribute existence in its true sense to the basic particles, it is also problematic for us to treat matter as having existence in its real meaning. It is for this reason that on different occasions during the past years, doubts

---

1. Ibid., p. 206.

2. Erwin Rudolf Josef Alexander Schrüdinger (1887 – 1961): a physicist and theoretical biologist who was one of the fathers of quantum mechanics. [Trans.]

3. Mahdi Golshani, An Analysis of the Philosophical Viewpoints of Contemporary Physicists), p. 245.

about the current expression of the quantum theory have been voiced by dialectical materialists. But, it (dialectical materialism) has not been able to present an essentially new expression from the perspective of the quantum theory... There is no dispute in that modern basic particles are nearer to the Platonic systematic bodies than Democritus' atoms. Modern basic particles are determined by means of the requirements of mathematical symmetry such that they become similar to the systematic bodies in the philosophy of Plato. They are permanent and inalterable, and therefore, they can hardly be considered real in the usual sense of the word; rather, they must be regarded as simple structural display of basic mathematics, which we can reach. In modern natural science there is no such thing but [only] form; it is mathematical symmetry. The origins are also things. And, since mathematical structure in the end is nothing but a rational substance, it can thus be said, in the words of Goethe:[1] "In the beginning I was thinking... It is interesting for me that at the present time, in all parts of the globe, and with all the technological means at our disposal, man strives and solves problems which the Greek philosophers presented 2,500 years ago, and we will know the answers within a few years' time in the future or at least within the next two decades."[2]

84. James Jeans – Matter as a mere subjective concept:

The world cannot allow physical display and the reason behind, in my opinion, is that it has become a mere subjective concept.[3]

85. Niels Bohr:

"In the great stage play of existence, we are both performers and spectators" as quoted from Laozi. Bohr believes that the function of science is not only to know the nature of things and to provide

---

1. Johann Wolfgang von Goethe (1749-1832): German poet, novelist, and playwright. [Trans.]

2. Mahdi Golshani, An Analysis of the Philosophical Viewpoints of Contemporary Physicists), pp. 197-198.

3. Ibid., p. 37.

a description of the external world; rather, its [other] function is to establish the relationship between and among various human experiences. Therefore, whenever we talk about the description of nature, we do not mean a description of nature independent from human beings. In fact, we mean human experiences... it is wrong for us to think that the function of physics is to discover the essence of nature. Physics has something to do with what we can say about nature.[1]

86. Arthur Fine:[2]

Realism is dead ...[3] Faine claims that he himself is neither realist nor anti-realist but rather treading a third path which refrains from talking about the external world or giving an analysis of the notion of the truth. Here, his contention is that talking about them must be discarded because of their lack of meaning, or irrelevance. In fact, he says that we discard them because there is no reference to solve these disputes. This outlook of Fine can be regarded as caused by his philosophical despair.[4]

We can say that in view of the three reasons and proving the reality of things while setting aside the perception of the perceiver, Fine's claim that "Realism is dead" is a negative philosophical premise because the need to establish that realism is alive, one cannot set aside realistic discussions and studies.

We must not forget the fact that in knowing the truths of the universe, sometimes the straightest lines are the longest, most complex and most curvy. It is good for Fine to know that if the need for many investigations in knowing the realities of the universe hindered thinking about them, then mankind would not have achieved the advancement we can see.

---

1. Ibid., pp. 80-81.

2. Arthur Fine (born 1937): an American philosopher of science teaching at the University of Washington (UW). [Trans.]

3. Mahdi Golshani, An Analysis of the Philosophical Viewpoints of Contemporary Physicists), p. 198.

4. Ibid., pp. 198-199.

87. Weisskopf:[1]

It is true that an unambiguous description of atomic reality with usual concepts of the physical process is impossible, but we have an unambiguous mathematical design that provides correct prediction and probability for observation.[2]

88. Carl Friedrich von Weizsäcker[3]:

With the theory of historical evolution of atomic physics, the sciences of chemistry and physics have been fused into a single unit. Since atom is the common bedrock of both sciences, other sciences such as astronomy, aerology, geology, and mineralogy deal with even the description and classification of phenomena for the explanation and establishment of legitimacy. Nowadays, this constitutes the area of application of each of the fundamental sciences of chemistry and physics. Moreover, physics and chemistry have become essential supporting means in organic science.

The concept of atom can be considered a tied spot in the scientific fabric of truth. The experiences of the various branches of science revolve around this tied spot, thereby connecting them together. Chemistry alone, knowledge of heat alone, or the mere theory about protons only makes the existence of atoms probable. That which joins together the threads of different arguments of these principles in claiming the existence of atoms, or what these threads have produced particularly in this case is what I have called 'scientific fabric'. The possibility of correctness of the final results with such coordination of the compacted and sown lines

---

1. Victor Frederick Weisskopf (1908 – 2002): an Austrian born Jewish American theoretical physicist. [Trans.]

2. Zum Weltbild der Physik, Leipzig 1946.

Its English translation is The World View of Physics, London, 1952. [Trans.]

3. Carl Friedrich Freiherr von Weizsäcker (1912-2007) was a German physicist and philosopher. He was the longest-living member of the team which performed nuclear research in Germany during the Second World War, under Werner Heisenberg's leadership (Ed.)

is as irreducible as it grows and reaches more tied spots.[1]

---

1. Mahdi Golshani, An Analysis of the Philosophical Viewpoints of Contemporary Physicists),. pp. 198-199.

Chapter 5
On Essential Reality

Eastern and Western Scholars on the Essential Reality

At the outset, it must be borne in mind that, in view of the three fundamental principles and religious way of thinking, the collective view of hundreds of thinkers on the reality of "the thing in itself", can be identified. Those three principles are as follows:

First Principle – Human knowledge (both scientific and philosophical) is the product of the reality of the thing in itself and the qualitative effect of the faculties of one's perception of the said reality, except in two cases: (1) self-consciousness (intuitive knowledge) and (2) understanding the concept of God. This is because our knowledge in these two cases is not in need of the agency of various elements of preconceived feelings and principles, particular stance and specific orientation. Thus, all questions of science and philosophy are a product of the relationship of "I with its elements of perception" or "other than I".

Second Principle: There is a direct and indirect relationship of the phenomena and components of the world with one another. The existence of something unknown in the world of nature is sufficient to prove that no rational person can ever claim to understand all things by means of pure science! Our knowledge, in contrast to what we do not know is such that the likes of Newton have said, "We are like small children standing by a vast ocean and can see only a small amount of sand on the shore!"

Third Principle: We cannot grasp the real nature of things and our knowledge cannot go beyond knowing the logical nature of things. ˉadr al-Muta'allihīn Shīr¡zī defines philosophy as "the knowledge of the truths of existents as far as human comprehension can reach." It is the same principle we have just mentioned because the truth from which the intrinsic order of real nature stems, is unknowable.

Keeping these three principles in view, the claim that one can know the realities of the world of nature 'as they are' through science and philosophy is not convincingly proved. The positivists do not consider the reality of things except as it is knowable. Bohemia says, "There is two fundamental points that quantum theory does not deal with: (1) the existence of things: quantum theory states that nothing can be examined except the possibility of a thing which can be observed if instruments are utilized; (2) anything which practically takes place." Concerning fundamental questions, the positivists are of the opinion that existence necessitates the use of concepts, which are actually undefinable and thus must be avoided.[1]

In this discourse we shall present the views of many of the most famous philosophers and scientists—both in the past and the present, the East and West—and find out who, among them, regard the essential reality of nature as unfathomable disregarding the abovementioned three principles.

The Main Views of Philosophers and Scholars on the Essential Reality of Things

1. *Rational truths are beyond perceptible things.* Some philosophers have also used the term 'Universal Intellect' for it. Among those who expressed this view are the following:

(1) Plato, (2) Samkhya, (3) Hindu concept of the unity of beings, (4) Heraclides, (5) Zeno, (6) Parmenides, (7) Marcus Aurelius Antoninus, (8) Meister Eckhart, (9) Hegel, (10) Alfred Fuillie, (11) Nicolas Malebranche, (12) Davies, and (13) Jalil al-Dīn Muḥammad Mawlawī Rumi.

It is impossible to prove the rational truth beyond the perceptible things through reason and to state its nature through sensory perceptions and scientific experiments. The perceptible things are in a state of constant change and our perceptions about them are relative. Therefore, proving rational truth as the foundation of those perceptible things cannot be correct. In order to prove this point, some Qur'ịnic verses may be cited; for

---

1. Mahdi Golshani, An Analysis of the Philosophical Viewpoints of Contemporary Physicists),. p. 33.

example:

> *Everyone in the heavens and the earth asks Him. Every day He is engaged in some work.*[1]

2. *The essential reality of things is unknown.* All the thinkers who believe in the real nature of things as unknown, such as the Muslim philosophers and scholars, also believe in the essential reality of things as unknown. Among these Muslim scholars are Ibn Sīnį, Fįrįbī, Ibn Rushd, Bahmanyįr, Muḥammad ibn Zakariyyį Rįzī, Īrįnshahrī, Khwįjah Naȳīr al-Dīn al-±ūsī, Mīr Dįmįd, ‾adr al-Muta'allihīn Shīrįzī, and Mīr Findiriskī. Positivist thinkers also believe that the essential reality of things is unknown.

Among the thinkers who believe in the essential reality of things as unknown are Kant, Felicite Robert de Lamennais, Herbert Spencer, Heron von Helmholtz, Blaise Pascal, Max Planck, John Locke, Maine de Biran, Comte, Bernard Bolzano, Voltaire, George Santayana, Joseph de Meister, Antoine Kernu, Oliver Lodge, Schopenhauer, Jean Filo, Baruch Spinoza, William Hamilton, Thomas Carlyle, and Heidegger.

Hippolyte Taine says that acquiring perception of the essential reality of things is impossible but he himself has not defined it. Yet, can these principles be proved by science or something else? Emile Boutroux, Umov, Oswald Külpe, Albert Einstein, Weisskopf, Arthur Fine, Weizsäcker, Bernard d'Espagnat (who describes the essential reality of things as 'veiled reality'), and Schrodinger share the same view. These [last] two thinkers also consider the essential reality of things comprehensible but they have not yet presented the scientific way to attain it. Schrodinger is famous for this statement: "Modern science is as far as the science of the ancient Greeks in discovering the laws of nature."[2] So, he can also be included in this group.

---

1. Sŧrat al-Raḥmįn 55:29.

2. Mahdi Golshani, An Analysis of the Philosophical Viewpoints of Contemporary Physicists), p. 245,

3. *Indivisible particles in the mental realm are the Reality*. Among those who support this view are Democritus and Leucippus.[1]

4. *Water is the Reality*. Thales must be mentioned as one of those who subscribe to this view.

5. *Air is the Reality*. Among those who support this view are Anaximenes, Diogenes Laertius and Archelaus.

6. *Numbers and extension of subject in theoretical geometry is the Reality*. The supporters of this view are personalities like Pythagoras and René Descartes.

7. *Matter and form are the Reality*: Of the supporters of this view, the names of such figures as Anaxagoras, St. Bonaventure, and all proponents of prime matter.

8. *The primary truth (genus) is the Reality*. Arthrina (?) is among the proponents of this view.

It is clear that each of these things claimed to be the essential reality of things—in view of the mental state of the respective claimants—has received considerable attention. For example, numbers for Pythagoras is the most pervasive truth in the world of nature, present as the essential reality of existents. For this reason, Pythagoras regarded the world as understandable through a mathematical lens. In the same manner, Descartes would look at the world through a geometrical lens, and these two thinkers focus on the detached quantity (number) and attached quantity (extension). When Pythagoras said, "The world of nature is a prison for man," he was probably referring to the pervasiveness of quantity, which encompasses all levels of this world. But, he has not been mentioned to have indicated number as the reason behind this world being the prison for man. Jal¡l al-Dīn Mu!ammad Mawlawī (Rūmī) has expressed this correlation in a very elegant literary style:

---

1. Leucippus or Leukippos (first half of 5th century BCE): one of the earliest Greeks to develop the theory of atomism – the idea that everything is composed entirely of various imperishable, indivisible elements called atoms – which was elaborated in greater detail by his pupil and successor, Democritus. [Trans.]

O God, reveal to the soul that place where speech is growing without letters,

That the pure soul may make of its head a foot towards the far-stretching expanse of non-existence —

An expanse very ample and spacious; and from it this phantasy and being is fed.

Imagination is narrower than non-existence: therefore, phantasy is the cause of pain.

Existence, again, is narrower than Imagination: hence, in it, moons become like the moon that has waned.

Again, the existence of the world of sense and colour is narrower, for it is a narrow prison.

The cause of narrowness is composition and number: the senses are moving towards composition.

Know that the world of Unification lies beyond sense: if you want Unity, march in that direction.[1]

Among these limited and general concepts, atoms, primary water and air are more indicative of the reality outside the human essence, but the limitation of their identities is convincingly applicable to the entire world of nature. Yet, science has not accepted any of the abovementioned concepts as the essential reality of things.

9. *Living particles (monads)*: Giordano Bruno, Leibniz, Herbert Spencer, Jean-Marie Guyau, Hermann Lotze, and Fechner are among the proponents of this view.

This view is also cited from some philosophical schools of thought such as Hylozoism, which holds that prime matter possesses life, and it is also believed by those who support the impossibility of producing life from a non-living entity (animate from inanimate), as substantiated by scientific and philosophical reasoning. Qur'¡nic verses point out this notion that all beings sing the glory of God; for example, this passage:

Whatever there is in the heavens glorifies Allah and

---

1. Rumi's *Masnavi*, Book 1, lines 3092-3099, pp. 333, 335. [Trans.]

whatever there is in the earth.[1]

And the reason for this is as follows:

> *The entity that has not been endowed with existence*
>
> *How to others could it be the endower of existence*
>
> *The cloud that is void of water*
>
> *It can not be the water giver*
>
> *That who lacks something cannot give it.*

A scientific reason is acceptable because that which does not have life—assuming that it must give life—is clearly a contradictory proposition. If matter does not possess the origin of life, living things coming into existence from it is a contradiction not permitted by any philosophical school or scientific law.

10. *Reality is discernable by the human mind*. The supporters of this view are Copernicus, George Berkeley,[2] Boscovich John Dewey, and Nietzsche.

Although this group of thinkers has diverse opinions, they all agree that the mind that can discern the reality, which necessitates its concrete existence. It seems farfetched to dismiss the very essential reality of things with the requisite of the channel of the senses and mental faculty, and to say that if the mind does not perceive a thing, it follows that it does not exist![3]

---

1. S£rat al-Jum'ah 62:1; S£rat at-Tagh¡bun 64:1.

2. George Berkeley, also known as Bishop Berkeley (1685 – 1753): an Anglo-Irish philosopher whose primary achievement was the advancement of a theory he called "immaterialism" (later referred to as "subjective idealism" by others), which denies the existence of material substance and instead contends that familiar objects are only ideas in the minds of perceivers, and as a result cannot exist without being perceived. [Trans.]

3. Given this, in my book Mawlaw¢ wa Jah¡nb¢n¢h¡ (R£m¢ and Worldviews), I have presented three reasons for dismissing idealism, which I shall mention here due to their importance in this discourse.

First reason – the unity of perception and the diversity of the perceived with this explanation that the idealist must be told: The function of the eyes is to see appearances of shapes, colors and others, and this is a phenomenon or activity which is the exclusive function of the eyes. We can see when we look at a chair; we can see that the specific shape of the chair is not a pen; it is not a piece of bread; it is not a sea; it is not an apple either. When one looks at each of the mentioned things, he can see its specific shape and color and not any other thing. If these things have diverse reality in the concrete world outside the sight, then from where does the diversity in our viewpoints originate? Moreover, the function of the mind which is to reflect the existents and appearances in the concrete world is nothing but a phenomenon and that is reflecting concrete things. So, from where do all these differences in the reflected things originate?

Second reason – the reality or truth that wavers between itself and other than itself can never be possible. Without doubt, that which is real is a specific thing in reality (although the way of proving it is my perception) and not any other thing which wavers between itself and other than itself. For example, from a distance I can see an object in the desert and I do not know if it is a stone or a person. That which is real is either a stone and not a person, or a person and not a stone. Due to the distance from the object, I am not sure if it is a stone or a person but in reality one of them is definite and not indefinite. And idealist can even say that what I can see is a thing whose reality is uncertain! If ever he makes such a claim, then he is not a world-viewer but a self-viewer whose ideal place is the coffeeshops of the Sophists during the ancient time. It is this idealist which cannot prove his own self which has no reflection in his own mind.

The idealists may possibly cite the lack of definite new physical form and say: "In today's conceptual and fundamental atomic issues, event or happening is definite and prior to the occurrence of an event, we cannot see anything definite about it." In reply to this, first of all, if in our knowledge and understanding, we follow the conclusion 'I cannot see it, therefore it does not exist,' then we must dispose of the subjects in psychology, psychotherapy and psychoanalysis because none of the psychological phenomena, my activities and myself which are important fundamental truths of those sciences can be seen. Can we say that they do not exist?! Secondly, an event which is happening has a definite state at every point in the process and after manifesting itself at a certain point, it will have the same definite state although for an observer the same latest point, prior to the occurrence of the event, will be determined with wider possibilities. I do not why they are so frightened by this statement, "The world has an identity beyond itself."

Third reason – man's necessity for having stances vis-à-vis the realities apart from himself. Let us explain. The coldness of weather compels him to wear warm clothes. He is runs away from a beast of prey. He changes his direction when there is a hole in front of him. He looks for light in order to see an object. These

11. *The essential reality of things is an abstraction of the "ego"*. The role of the "ego" in the philosophy of Fichte is identical with the role of the "mind" in the philosophy of Hegel. With the expression that "The ego established itself and therefore it equally established the non-ego," it follows that the entire universe is a result of the establishment of both the ego and the non-ego. This thought helps in comprehending the greatness of the ego, but there is no scientific proof that the essential reality is only the "ego" or that essential reality emanates from the "ego".

12. *The "ego" and "non-ego"*: Schelling says, "The world and the ego, whether subjective or objective, are of one nature and emanate from the same origin." Since Schelling acknowledges the existence of another power in nature different from outward concrete powers and the power in the soul also exists in nature, it can be said that his theory also cannot be studied through pure science in the so-called contemporary period.

11. Substantial Matter consists of matter and intellect, particularly its mathematical activity, and this matter has no attached extension. Bertrand Russell, Heisenberg and Niels Bohr are among the supporters of this theory.

These figures and their likes regard the essential reality of things as a two-dimensional reality (subjective or intelligible, and objective). Has the advancement in science and technology been directly premeditated by philosophers, logicians and scientists with a specific orientation in relation to the desired results so that all the scientific and technological processes and their outcomes have been realized with utmost precision and logical pattern?

Our main problem concerning the relationship of science with the realities in the universe is not the exact knowledge of the technical nature of science, which, nowadays, has

---

stances vis-à-vis is the best proof of the permanence of the reality apart from oneself. Man knows that realities are in contact with him whether he can perceive them or not. As can be observed, in explaining the criterion for the essential reality of things, the school of idealism does not also cite science to support its claim. In fact, science is inconsistent with this school of thought.

preoccupied our minds. This is because scientific discoveries [and invenstions] in the ancient world and in the last two centuries have made humanity triumph in the realms of both science and technology. Nowadays, most discoverers [and inventors] either do not have the necessary information about the technical discourses and terms in science (such as universality in its abstract sense, predictability, unfalsifiability, experimentation, observation, and their stages and conditions), or their information is insufficient. At any rate, they have introduced abundant discoveries [and inventions] into the domain of science. For example, Thomas Edison[1] who has been credited with approximately 950 inventions, Pasteur[2] with extraordinary inventions, and Nobel,[3] with over 350 patents under his name (and despite the lack of formal secondary and tertiary level education) had no professional expertise in the respective branches of science. In fact, they also did not have totally extensive and accurate knowledge of the respective branches of science compared to the professtional experts. Of course, direct and indirect endeavor and quest for the realities are an essential requisite of discovering and inventing. In order to elaborate this point, we shall cite the case of a very famous personality, viz. Hermann von Helmholtz (1821 – 1894).

Of the three physicists mentioned by Planck in 1935, Helmholtz is the most famous. He is one of the multi-talented scholars that the world has so far produced. Of course, he cannot be regarded as a mere physicist because he had neither formal education nor any degree in physics. And until 1871 when he accepted the offer of professorship in physics at the Berlin

---

1. Thomas Alva Edison (1847 – 1931): an American inventor, scientist, and businessman who developed many devices that greatly influenced life around the world, including the phonograph, the motion picture camera, and a long-lasting, practical electric light bulb. [Trans.]

2. Louis Pasteur (1822-95): a French chemist and microbiologist who was a pioneer in pasteurization and the use of vaccines. [Trans.]

3. Alfred Bernhard Nobel (1833 – 1896): a Swedish chemist, engineer, innovator, and armaments manufacturer. [Trans.]

University—that is, the most credible position in German physics—he had never officially taught physics before. Helmholtz has also important works in medicine, physiology, chemistry, mathematics, philosophy, and linguistics. Notwithstanding this, he always considered himself as an "inborn physicist", and given the numerous great works he had in physics, he truly deserved the title.

Heinrich Hertz,[1] the most renowned student of Helmholtz, has described his share in research, thus:

> Delving into the details, as the perculiarity of all research studies of Helmholtz, is futile. If whatever will be omitted in writing be divided among some men of knowledge, this will be sufficient for all of them to become famous! If a scientist had only done Helmholtz's research in the field of electricity, we could have regarded him as one of the cream of the crop in electricity. If one of the people of knowledge had not done anything except discover the laws of circular motion of fluid, he could have boasted of attaining one of the most elegant discoveries in mechanics.
>
> If a person would have presented the same reflections of Helmholtz on the acquired and real peculiarities of space, no one could have denied that he is endowed with the blessing of ingenuity in mathematics. But the awareness that all these discoveries, that belong to some individuals, actually belong to a single person is a source of delight for us. The possession of these feats by a single person falsifies the accidental nature of each of them.
>
> We consider these achievements a proof of the existence of a gifted person who goes far beyond our capabilities. And our knowing this elicits our praise... Undoubtedly, for the span of 23 years, from 1871 until his death, Helmholtz was a forerunner of German physics, leading the scientific development in Germany and reaching an outstanding status in the world at the

---

1. Heinrich Rudolf Hertz (1857 – 1894): a German physicist who clarified and expanded the electromagnetic theory of light that had been put forth by Maxwell. [Trans.]

end of the nineteenth century. His colleagues recognized his lone status and, due to the love they had for the station of a single person, they have adoringly recognized him as the imperial honor in German physics.1

In view of the appearance of knowledge and discoveries, we arrive at the conclusion that the efforts of the professional experts of the positivists and logicians are nothing but organizing the realities after their appearance in the arena of knowledge, whose foundation is sometimes molded by their a priori principles. The outcome of this practice is more or less like organizing a bowl, plates, spoons, and forks on a dining table, and consciously or unconsciously, the people do not enter to select the food according to the arrangement on the table, table-spread or dining table for the elite. This is while the cooks prepare the food and drink.

This fact is acknowledged by approximately all the authorities in the field of discoveries and inventions. In his introduction to Experimental Medicine, Claude Bernard thus explains:

No rule or order can stipulate that at the time of observing a particular object, a correct and fruitful idea, which is a sort of prior mental guideline for correct research, would come to the mind of the researcher. It is only after the idea came to the mind that one sees how it must be consistent with specific stipulations of logical rules, which must not be violated by any researcher. But the cause of its emergence is unknown and its nature completely personal, and it is something special, which is considered the source of initiative, invention and ingenuity of every person.[2]

Alfred North Whitehead argues,

That we must think in order to attain the truths is something

1. Majalleh-ye Fiz¢k, no. 1, pp. 1-4 (Originally in Persian).

2. Felicien Challaye, Shinįkht-e Rawishhį-ye 'Ul£m (Knowing the Scientific Methods), trans Yahyį Mahdawₜ, p. 42 (originally in French).

> *exactly contrary to the reality, because a great deal of*
> *advancements (discoveries and inventions) have not been a*
> *product of organized thoughts.[1]*

The most fundamental pillar of discoveries is undoubtedly and categorically intuition or inspiration. At most, there is a difference of opinion on its explanation. A group of great thinkers of both the East and the West believe that inspiration is a divine phenomenon. Among those who belong to this group are Socrates, Plato, Carlyle, Sorokin,[2] and Marie Tien. George F. Kneller says, "One of the oldest concepts is creationism, which revolves around the axis that the Creator possesses a divine inspiration. Without doubt, this concept bespeaks of the extraordinary initiative involved in great masterpieces of the creator. This concept is basically mentioned by Plato, who stated that at the time of creating something, since he is not in control of himself, the artist is influenced by a superior force. According to Plato, Socrates says to Ion the Poet, 'The gift which you possess of speaking excellently… is not an art, but, as I was just saying, an inspiration; there is a divinity moving you.'[3] This viewpoint that the artist acquires inspiration from a supra-human power is also prevalent today. For example, Sorokin believes that the greatest findings of the Creator are a product of supernatural-super-sensory power. The power he conceives at the time of creating [something] is highly unknown and transcends beyond our consciousness. Marie Tien expresses that creationism emanates from beyond nature. The creator's power is based upon knowing the existence of an unconscious or semi-conscious mind which Plato and other men of wisdom were aware of, and inattention to this point under the mere pretext of Freudian self-

---

1. Sargudhasht-e And¢shehh¡ (Adventures of Ideas).

2. Pitirim Alexandrovich Sorokin (1889 – 1968): was a Russian-American sociologist best known for his contributions to the social cycle theory. [Trans.]

3. Plato, Ion, trans. Benjamin Jowett, available online at

  http://classics.mit.edu/Plato/ion.html. [Trans.]

unconsciousness is a sign of lack of wisdom of our time."[1]

If the phenomenon of intuition or inspiration were scientifically explicable then, just as chess players (and not the realists) claim scientific improvements, the history of knowledge and science would have been definitely more glorious than we have are currently treading.

Those who, on account of extreme allergy to the word 'science' and its derivatives, want to deny every fact which is outside their mental perimeter must know that if intuition, illumination, inspiration and the like were beyond the interpretation and analysis of pure science, then

1. We were not supposed to be in our present state of knowledge;

2. It is clear that given such a premise (that intuition, illumination, and inspiration are beyond scientific interpretation and analysis), we could have prevented all errors which caused intellectual and financial losses, wasting of time and digression from the direction of science and learning. Yet, unfortunately, it can be said that the number of errors in the theories and in that which is scientific are far more than what is normal. We have encountered a lot of such expressions as "This hypothesis has been proved by experiment" and "There is no doubt on this issue from the scientific viewpoint." Of course, subsequent experiments, observations and other methods of research have proven their invalidity.

3. If it were possible for us to totally manage intuition, illumination and inspiration, certainly we could have managed development, progress and enhancement of science and knowledge in a direct fashion with more intelligible orientations.

Upon these discussions, we arrive at this very important conclusion that the principles and fundamentals of scientific hypotheses are based upon intuition, illumination and inspiration which are beyond science. That is, non-scientific

---

1. George F. Kneller, Hunar wa 'Ilm wa Khaliqiyyat (Art, Science and Creativity), trans. Dr. Sayyid 'Ali A¥ghar Musaddad, pp. 20-21.

phenomena shape scientific hypotheses and make them practically beneficial.

Attention paid to the account of discoveries and innovations will serve as a good guideline for us. You can come across the following points in the history of technology and inventions:

For many of the different inventions, nay even far more, there is no point in urging that, in the period of history we talk about, all technological devices and machines have been more or less based upon unsystematic and haphazard method. In order to determine the necessary thickness for constructing a column, or to design the half body of a ship, or to compute the height of a waterfall, which is supposed to turn the wheel of the watermill, the engineers at that time could not apply the modern engineering method. That is, there were no general rules at that time and all their knowledge consisted of a set of experiences throughout many centuries and periods and were applied randomly. It is exactly like the Sumerian people who, in every state or condition for the period of four thousand years, had a specific prescription at their disposal according to their past experiences. These pieces of knowledge had never been inferred from the theoretical principles taught in schools...[1]

***

The industry during the period of modernity can never be likened to the set of systematic innovations which is the single source of all cases of utility. In fact, on the contrary, it can be regarded as an effusion of each of the inventions without any relation with one another—inventions which are a product of intuition and the exigency of time.[2]

***

The extraordinary effusion of this kind of invention, devoid of any importance and only a product of inspirations and

---

1. Pierre Rousseau, Histoire des techniques et des inventions, (originally in French).

2. Ibid., p. 190.

exigencies of time, will appear uncoordinated to us when we see that a set of irrational activities, consistent with the norm of that period, were also carried out; for example, the pursuit for the eternal (immortality, alchemy, water of life, etc.). This was one such astounding craft, solely based upon the simplest experiments, whose main element was mere acquisition of literacy and its application, and carried out without any sort of scientific concepts. Even in most of the mentioned cases, usual criticism did not serve as a guide. Without doubt, it proved the presence of a kind of sagacity and dexterity, but it was impossible for it to provide us the way of attaining universal or general advancements.[1]

***

At that time, this passionate and profound soul (Denis Papin[2]) had been more than ever engrossed in thinking about the power of water vapor. The perculiarity of the problem was that due to the passage of time, the nature of the problem expanded and changed in his view. In the beginning, Denis Papin had only in his mind a simple technique of bringing up the water from a mineral well, but gradually the horizon turned wider for him. The said inventor rightly guessed that beyond the problem of bringing up water from a mineral well was possibly the generation of an extensive source of energy, which could be used in bringing up water from a mineral well and pumping, or setting a new vehicle and a sewing machine, ship and means of public transport.[3]

Max Planck said,

Imagine a miner who for many years was digging the ground in search for minerals. But one night he found a grain of gold which

---

1. Ibid., p. 192.

2. Denis Papin (1647 - c. 1712): a French-born physicist, mathematician and inventor, best known for his pioneering invention of the steam digester, the forerunner of the steam engine and the pressure cooker. [Trans.]

3. Pierre Rousseau, Histoire des techniques et des inventions.

he never expected. It is somehow clear that if he had not found this grain of gold, somebody else would have found it.[1]

There are very important ups and downs in the course of science which are caused by the commission of errors and mistakes in the realm of science.

---

1. Ibid.

Chapter 6
The Limits of Science in Knowing the Reality

Opinion-survey for Identifying the Reality in the Realm of Science!

"Nowadays, the physicists have a consensus of opinion that there is no consensus of opinion among them about the condition of cases in the microphysical world! In order to show the existing crisis in the thought of contemporary physicists, it is sufficient to pay attention to an opinion survey recently conducted at the end of a conference. This conference with the theme, "Microphysical Reality and Quantum Formalism", was held in the autumn of 1985 in Italy. One of the basic questions asked was: Is there another that exerts influence, or none? Einstein used to reject it (Einsteinian Position). At the conclusion of this conference, two of the physicists distributed the questionnaires among the participating physicists. The questions commenced with this introduction:

"This conference has shown that there are many differences in expressing quantum mechanics of recent experiments. The only way of getting out of this mental dilemma is to resort to statistical data. Therefore, we respectfully ask you to honestly answer the questions below."

Fifty-six of the participants answered the questions and we shall present here parts of the questions and answers:

Question: *Do you believe in the Einsteinian Position, i.e. the lack of possibility of signaling or influence with speed more than that of the speed of light?*

Answer: 54% = yes, 39% = no, 7% undecided

Question: *Do you believe that the recent experiments have invalidated the Einsteinian Position?*

Answer: 30% = yes, 57% = no, 13% undecided

Question: *Do you believe that the recent experiments on signaling have confirmed the Ultra Light?*

Answer: 5% = yes, 89% = no, 6% undecided

Question: *Do you think that the recent experiments have confirmed the influence of the Ultra Light?*
Answer: *21% = yes, 52% = no, 27% undecided*

> **Question:** *Do you think that a term for quantum mechanics has never been found like the one well chosen for the classical mechanic?*
>
> **Answer:** *71% = yes, 18% = no, 11% undecided*
>
> **Question:** *Are you a realist?*
>
> **Answer:** *86% = yes, 2% (one person) = no, 12% undecided*
>
> **Question:** *Do you believe that there is a world apart from this world (without considering the elements of your perception) after your death?*
>
> **Answer:** *98% = yes, 2% = no, 0% undecided*
>
> **Question:** *Is the glass transparent in a dark place?*
>
> **Answer:** *64% = yes, 9% = no, 27% undecided*
>
> **Question:** *Do you believe in a kind of phenomena above the mind, or magic?*
>
> **Answer:** *55% = yes, 18% = no, 27% undecided*

Notwithstanding the mental agitation existing in the views of contemporary physicists, the silence has been broken and fundamental questions have been raised again, more or less. There is strong hope that physics will be relieved from the veiled dogmatism engulfing it, and conception of the condition of the microphysical world will not only be explained but also the goal of the physicists theorized.

The state of affairs has been well summarized in this manner:

An increasing number of scientists have seriously questioned absolute credibility of quantum mechanics. This wariness has reached a point where the founders of quantum mechanics have left the theory in such a way that, though successful in practice, it seriously limits our intuitive knowledge of the microphysical world, and their reasons are, to a great extent, optional and questionable.[1]

1. Taịlẹlẹ az Dẹdgịh-hị-ye Falsafẹ-ye Fẹzẹkdịnịn-e Mu'ị¥ir (An Analysis of the Philosophical Viewpoints of Contemporary Physicists), 2nd edition, pp. 29-31 (originally in Persian)

Declaration of the Bankruptcy of Science*

It is said that in one of the cities in Germany, there was a ruler whose truthfulness and dedication were proverbial. Thieves and brigands were afraid of him while the upright people truly respected him. One day, however, the city dwellers got to know of a dreadful secret; that is, every night, the ruler would change his clothes and bring a pistol with him. He would surreptitiously get out of his house and rob people on the street, taking some items from them by force... Certainly, you would ask: is it not the same story of Halers the Ruler? Perhaps, it is so, but at the same time, the story of mathematics in the latter part of the nineteenth century is also the same.

For the past twenty centuries, the people submitted to it and toed its line. Everyone wanted it to practically interfere and correct him in the smallest matter if his actions were like an affront of the things sacred. But suddenly, the Eucledian principle showed a dismal weakness and the veneer of sanctity attached to it was violently extinguished. The familiar domain of common numbers was crushed by the avalanche of irrational and immeasurable numbers, and the edifice, which was so respected and revered, incurred serious cracks and damages.

But it was not only the great edifice of mathematics which incurred such serious cracks and damages. The entire magnificent castle of science met the same fate. The savage war against Weismann[1] and the barbaric campaign against Lamarck's[2] laws of inheritance of acquired characteristics (or

---

* Certainly, the extremism in scientism, which reaches the point of science-worship also includes such dissipation, but in our opinion, science cannot be the object of worship, nor is it bankrupt. In fact, these understandings of the reality can be shattered with the hatchet of "This is it and nothing else!" and this is ego-worship, which leads to the fall and failure of "I have progressed".

1. Friedrich Leopold August Weismann (1834 – 1914): a German evolutionary biologist. [Trans.]

2. Jean-Baptiste Pierre Antoine de Monet, Chevalier de la Marck, often just known as "Lamarck" (1744 – 1829): a French soldier, naturalist, academic and an

soft inheritance) commenced. By discovering quanta protons,
Planck had rendered a death blow to Leibniz's famous proverb
Natura non saltum facit (Law of Continuity)[1] and Becquerel[2]
discovered radioactivity. This recent concern, in particular,
turned the scientists' wandering into agitation, for it made them
face something completely uncommon. A simple element like
radium would set free another simple element like helium and
turn into a third element like radon. So, what is the main
function of Lavoisier's[3] principle? Nothing can be extinguished
and nothing can create its own self. Is this transformation of
radium into lead after undergoing certain processes not really
an affirmation of the laws of alchemy that have been ridiculed for
a long time? And a subject far more important than it is this:
what will happen to the principle of the subsistence of energy,
for it seems that the radiation produced by radioactive elements
is connected and inexhaustible? From where does this element
acquire this great source of energy?

In 1902, Rutherford[4] and Soddy[5] replied that the sources of this
energy are in the atoms of the element itself. These atoms
gradually explode or disintegrate and transmute into atoms of

---

early proponent of the idea that evolution occurred and proceeded in accordance with natural laws. [Trans.]

1. Introduced by Leibniz based on earlier work by Nicholas of Cusa and Johannes Kepler, the Law of Continuity which is expressed by the proverb Natura non saltum facit (Nature does not make a leap) is a heuristic principle that "whatever succeeds for the finite, also succeeds for the infinite". [Trans.]

2. Antoine Henri Becquerel (1852 – 1908): a French physicist, Nobel laureate, and the discoverer of radioactivity along with Marie Curie and Pierre Curie, for which all three won the 1903 Nobel Prize in Physics. [Trans.]

3. Antoine Laurent Lavoisier (1743-1794): French chemist, who is considered the founder of modern chemistry. [Trans.]

4. Ernest Rutherford (1871 – 1937): a New Zealand-born British chemist and physicist who became known as the father of nuclear physics. [Trans.]

5. Frederick Soddy (1877 – 1956): an English radiochemist who explained, with Ernest Rutherford, that radioactivity is due to the transmutation of elements, now known to involve nuclear reactions. [Trans.]

different kinds, and the produced energy is the result of the same disintegration. In reality, radioactivity signifies the death of atoms. It is certain that the scientists had not heartily welcomed such an explanation but, in any case, they entrusted it to fate, for classical physics and chemistry were in the process of extinction then. The principles on which, these two branches of science, were depending after Descartes, were fragmented and extinguished. The young generation wanted to expel the preceding generation, which, for it, was indeed pitiful, and it was perplexed and dumbfounded as to what must be done. The scientific methods, the philosophy of research and mechanical science, with the entire edifice of the theory of evolution, and whatever Spencer had added to it, were in shambles and crisis. As science as a whole was seriously threatened with bankruptcy, the scientists asked themselves: What shall be the function of today's knowledge? Is it destined to be wiped out at once or will there be something new to replace it?

Restrictions in Terms of Methodology and Objectives

Jules Henri Poincaré explained: "There are some elements in our thinking which we must select. For example, Euclidean geometry, Riemannian geometry and Lobachevskian geometry are of this sort. If we select the first geometry, it does not mean that the reality of this geometry is more than that of others. The reason, rather, is that this geometry is consistent with our experiences in the world. In other words, it is simpler compared to the other types of geometry. In the same manner, the declaration that the earth moves cyclically and that space has three dimensions is simpler compared to other similar principles." Pierre Duhem[1] (1861-1917), professor at the University of Bordeaux, also said: "Consistency with experience does not necessarily mean validity and correctness of a theory. All theories that gradually encompass the truth and are closer to

---

1. Pierre Maurice Marie Duhem (1861 – 1916): a French physicist, mathematician and philosopher of science, best known for his writings on the indeterminacy of experimental criteria and on scientific development in the Middle Ages. [Trans.]

it than ever before are correct by themselves." As the philosophers heard the scientists discuss audaciously the futility of knowledge and the lack of power of theories, they sharpened their ears and were informed of the failure of the major theories in mechanical science. But it was particularly astonishing for them that prominent figures like Poincaré and Duhem, experts in thermodynamics, could fiercely talk against the traditions of the nineteenth century. Around this time, the American philosopher William James (1842-1910) defined science in this way: "Science is a set of simple contracts." The Austrian philosopher Ernst Mach[1] (1838-1916) announced that after all stages, the animal body in reality is nothing but an apparatus of feelings and impressions. Finally, the class of enlightened and educated people totally changed its beliefs.

The extraordinary development of major industries, the spread of violent war initiated by the working class, the establishment of the Paris Commune,[2] and the great campaign launched against religion prompted the bourgeoisie to take the issue seriously and be engrossed in thinking. From the eighteenth century onward, this class presented itself as freedom-lovers, anti-cleric and advocate of Voltaire's ideas, insisting that it had emancipated itself from the shackles of old ideas and introduced itself as an advocate of modern revolutions. At the end of the nineteenth century, however, they also totally changed their ideas. They realized that all the enduring sanctities had been destroyed before their eyes. This generated intense fear in them and, like the student of a magician, they realised that they could no longer control the power which they had generated. As such, they looked for a pretext and suddenly declared that science was not able to do what Auguste Comte, Clyde Kluckhohn,

---

1. Ernst Mach (1838 – 1916): an Austrian physicist and philosopher. [Trans.]

2. Paris Commune: a government that briefly ruled Paris from March 18 to May 28, 1871 and hailed as the first assumption of power by the working class during the Industrial Revolution. [Trans.]

Helmholtz, and Berthelot[1] had attached to it. It must also be acknowledged that the simplicity and contempt of Haeckel's[2] transformism, the sudden collapse of the laws governing the principle of permanence of energy, the principle of the permanence of matter, and the vacuum which the discovery of x-ray, electron and radioactivity between modern thinking and classical knowledge had created, proved useful for advancing their goal. In 1859, Ferdinand Brunetière[3] (1849–1906) announced in Two Worlds Magazine the bankruptcy of science...[4]

The Balance Sheet of the School of Evolution

Obviously, from the time of Darwin[5] and De Vries[6] the question of evolution has changed a lot! Nowadays, we are as far from the mutationism of the year 1900 as from the transformism of the year 1860; the flaws of the school were disclosed so early. Initially, the theory of natural selection, insisted by Darwin, could not bring anything into being; rather, it only selected the most favorable of the gradual changes. Then, this question was raised: Why must some parts, such as the wings of Archaeopteryx, which were not fully developed and of no use,

---

1. Marcellin Pierre Eugène Berthelot (1827 – 1907): a French chemist and politician noted for the Thomsen-Berthelot principle of thermochemistry. [Trans.]

2. Ernst Heinrich Philipp August Haeckel, also written von Haeckel (1834 – 1919): an eminent German biologist, naturalist, philosopher, physician, professor and artist, who discovered, described and named thousands of new species, mapped a genealogical tree relating all life forms, and coined many terms in biology. [Trans.]

3. Ferdinand Brunetière (1849 – 1906): a French writer and critic. [Trans.]

4. History of Science, pp. (Originally in English).

5. Charles Robert Darwin (1809-82): English naturalist and one of the strongest and best-known defenders of organic evolution, whose most important work is The Origin of Species by Means of Natural Selection (1859). [Trans.]

6. Hugo Marie de Vries (1848 – 1935): a Dutch botanist and one of the first geneticists. [Trans.]

gradually develop? Moreover, it is as if the survival of the fittest theory in most cases is accidental in nature, and Morris Colleiry (?) added, "If we consider how many eggs and larvas of insects die in seas, it will be clear that the only factor that decides the survival of creatures is accident and nothing else!" The sudden changes which are mostly mentioned are only about the types and nothing else. It is never seen that a family or a class of creatures has turned into another family. Moreover, the animals or plants that are the outcome of sudden change are mainly the weak and inferior, and they can never be a good representation of the theory of survival of the fittest.

The lack of power of three grand theories, viz. Lamarckism, Darwinism and mutationism has prompted many of the researchers to propose new explanations. A German contemporary of Darwin named Moritz Wagner[1] (1813-1887) announced in 1875 a new theory which was very close to that of Lamarck, saying that "In my opinion, formation of new types is conditioned by geographical factors. Ernst Mayr[2] modified his view, saying, "I think although these changes depend on external factors, only on certain extent can they develop." Then, Lousti (?) from Holland said, "Perhaps it is necessary for us to look for the cause of evolution in the internal factors identified by Mendel."[3] Ganu from France expressed, "In my opinion, evolution takes place by means of 'a prior conformity'. Finally, in 1929, L. Viapleton (1861-1930) boldly and categorically said that if we basically believe in evolutionism, it is obvious that there are absolutely no forms of partition. The proof of this is that

---

1. Moritz Wagner (1813 – 1887): a German explorer, collector, geographer and natural historian. [Trans.]

2. Ernst Walter Mayr (1904 – 2005): one of the 20th century's leading evolutionary biologists, and also a renowned taxonomist, tropical explorer, ornithologist, historian of science, and naturalist. [Trans.]

3. Gregor Johann Mendel (1822 – 1884): an Austrian scientist and Augustinian friar who gained posthumous fame as the founder of the new science of genetics. [Trans.]

the family tree of living organisms in most cases has parallel branches and stems which can rarely be associated with a single root or origin. Transformism is nothing but an illusion and imagination.[1]

***

However, it seems that most of the paleontologists, who are more credible in expressing opinion on this subject, prefer Lamarckism over other proofs, and Professor Colleiry (?) did not hide his inclination to it. But his Lamarckism is modern, and conforms with the discovery of chromosomes and genes.

Madislon Pole and Dan Pivetar (?) say: "Darwin wanted to determine the produced changes on a complete being, and denying this point is like putting the cart before the horse."

According to the views of Weismann which were presented in 1919-1920, by E.G. Conklin (b. 1863), an American professor at Princeton University, one must look for the causes of changes of the species in the changes undergone by the sperm and primary cells. Conklin expressed it in this way: "All the peculiarities that will later manifest and develop in a complete being take place in the zygote."

It is clear that the issue will not just end up here and this question will linger on: What is the source of changes that take place in the zygote? An objection against these views is this: since the researcher has the knowledge and the experiment cannot be transferred by heredity, do you think this specific Lamarckism is not also a mistake?

How do you know? Yes, at present, it is not transferable but was it not possible that it was transferable at the beginning of the geological periods? In contrast to these long periods, our experiences are so limited! And it is very possible that at present, the sperm has found a means of resisting and opposing external changes.

Definitely, the issue is yet to be resolved. The more one delves –

---

1. Pierre Rousseau, History of Science.

into it, the more problems and ambiguities will surface. At any rate, if the problem of the mechanism of evolution is yet to be resolved, the issue itself is definitely doubtful. Another proof to it has been obtained through a study of the life of parasites which undergo drastic and definite changes.

As we know, parasitism refers to the state of an organism living at the expense of another organism such that it gradually exhausts and extinguishes the other organism, and this the same thing the worms in the stomach do to the human being and bindweeds to the plants.

As can be observed, when a parasite totally attaches itself to another organism which becomes the source of its nourishment, that organism turns weak and gradually dies.[1]

In one of pages of the book *History of Science*, this point is mentioned, thus:

Today, all discoveries will be discussed again leading towards the unity of matter. [2]

And we can read this heading:

The seat of authority of analysis has shaken. [3]

And this heading has been discussed:

The school of evolution faces problems. [4]

Has science reached the optimum depth and width of the realities in the universe that it has the final words about them all, at all times, under all conditions for mankind?

From the earlier discussions, we can arrive at the conclusion that science has never reached such depth and width and it will never have the final words about all realities in the universe for mankind.

---

1. Ibid.

2. Ibid.

3. Ibid.

4. Ibid.

God, the Glorious, says:

And you have not been given of the knowledge except a few [of you].[1]

He also says:

And say, 'My Lord! Increase me in knowledge'.[2]

It is also stated in another place:

Allah will raise those of you who have faith and those who have been given knowledge in rank, and Allah is well aware of what you do.[3]

First of all, before stating the limitation of science and its inability to delve into all dimensions of all the realities in the universe, we shall briefly touch on the greatness and necessity of science and life-giving power.

The seal of Solomon's kingdom is knowledge / The scholar's statement is the form and soul of knowledge.

Now, the hope-giving breezes of man's ardent desire to revive the lofty human values in the arena of human life by God's favor have started blowing.

Now, the all-encompassing sun of Divine religion has appeared from behind the artificial clouds of the ignorant and egoistic domineers, thereby waking the sleepy ones on earth by its early morning touches. Now, by presenting the quantities and qualities of its utility in the vast realm of the universe, science has come forward to remove the allegation of its being against religion. Now, the inhuman objectives of the egoists have been exposed. Now, the veils, covering the claims and pretensions of the group feigning support for science, have been lifted.

Now, by accurately identifying and assessing these two magnificent truths, the perspicacious scholars and authorities of both religion and science have sincerely and categorically declared the necessity for perfecting man's "intelligible life" by

1. Sūrat al-Isrāʾ (or Banū Isrāʾīl) 17:85.

2. Sūrat Ṭā Hā 20:114.

3. Sūrat al-Mujādilah 58:11.

means of coordinating science and religion. It is only proper that along this path which leads to the real felicity of man, more serious and expansive steps must be taken without any delay, and the thick veils, placed by the anti-religion and science ignoramuses or geniuses, on the real face of science and religion be lifted up.[1]

By quoting these everlasting words of Max Plack, who is undoubtedly one of the fathers of the 20th century science, we shall conclude the primary introduction:

"Concerning the relationship between religion and science, we must also state that the objection against religion, that it denies life, is not consistent with the perspective of science and contradictory to its principles. Any denial of the value of life is a denial of human thinking, and therefore, in the final analysis, it is not only denial of the real nature of science but also denial of religion itself. I think more scientists agree with my view and they will raise their hands of agreement with the fact that religious nihilism is also destructive to science.

> There will never be any real conflict between science and religion. Each of them is complementary to the other. Every serious person and thinker will be aware that if all the powers of human beings are supposed to be utilized in coordination and harmony with one another, one must acknowledge the existence of a religious element in his nature and strive hard to nourish it. And it is not accidental that the great thinkers in all periods have

---

1. The story of science and religion is like that of two extremely kind brothers who had been separated from each other for sometime and gradually each of them adopted the customs and appearance of the place where he lived in although they were really looking for each other. As a result, each of them assumed an appearance unfamiliar and antagonistic to the other. When the people of the two places where each of them lived waged war against each other, the two brothers also faced each other in the battlefield. As they got closer in a fight, they recognized each other and threw away their respective swords. They embraced each other and on account of the considerable clout each of them had, the two warring groups (rigid scientists and ritualistic religious devotees) were reconciled and thereafter they live together in peace and harmony.

been profound religious figures, even if they have not so much expressed religiousity.[1]

Five Reasons behind the Necessity and Greatness of Science

It is obvious that among the reasons behind the necessity for, and greatness of, science, five of them are preeminent and more important:

First reason: The astonishing activities and results of the extensive, in-depth and relative knowledge in the realm of the four types of relationships, which have been so far at the disposal of humanity.

Second reason: Science deals only with that which is within its domain of expertise and explores it through its specific tools. With this destructive statement, "I do not accept as reality except that which I can see," science will never undermine its credibility and value, for science is aware that for discovering the realities, the tools that it usually utilizes are natural senses, laboratories and mental activities of the scientist. Given its structural peculiarities and the environmental conditions of the elements of perception and special goals, colored realities—and not the realities as they are—are presented to the scientist. In all branches of science, we can clearly see this very meaningful and enduring statement, "In the great stage play of existence, we are both performers and spectators" as elucidated today by the authorities, ancient and modern, Eastern and Western, from Laotzi the Chinese philosopher to Robert Oppenheimer[2] the Westerner. And for this, we do not see any need for citation and reasoning.

Third reason: By distinguishing the realities in the arena of existence as being or non-being, science does not deal with do's and don'ts, although the ways of finding out their reality are

---

1. Max Planck, Where is Science Going?, (originally in English).

2. Julius Robert Oppenheimer (1904 – 1967): an American theoretical physicist and professor of physics who is often called the "father of the atomic bomb" for his role in the Manhattan Project, the World War II project that developed the first nuclear weapons. [Trans.]

different from one another. By considering what science seeks in the realities and that the do's and don'ts are also part of the realities, the said distinction is a kind of opposition to science. In the end, by proving them real, science will emerge victorious.

In order to accept the strength of this reason, we must scrutinize the statement of Max Planck, quoted to substantiate the fourth reason.

Fourth reason: As our knowledge and understanding of the laws governing the universe increase, the universe's sanctity also increases, for,which, two basic conditions are necessary:

First condition – faith in our existence in a meaningful world based on a sublime goal, as lucidly demonstrated by this Qur'¡nic verse:

> **Indeed we belong to Allah, and to Him do we indeed return.**[1]

Second condition – knowledge of the realities in the universe.

In order to acknowledge the greatness and sanctity of science, we shall only cite the statements of Max Plack:

> *It is through the cooperation between understanding and willpower that the finest fruit of philosophy can be found and this fruit is nothing but morality. Science enhances life through the moral values, thereby acquiring the love for the truth and the sacred—love for the truth about us which manifests in the incessant struggle to acquire a more accurate knowledge about the material and spiritual world, and love for the sacred in the sense that any advancement in knowledge places us before our existence.*[2]

Fifth reason: The crucial role of science in defending its original identity by, gradually, presenting the realities. It is an essential proposition that real science refers to the clarification of a reality with which the scientist has established connection. Real science is that whose clarification of a reality is perfect. A lack of

---

1. S£rat al-Baqarah 2:156.

2. Max Planck, Where is Science Going?.

just 1 % of the desired clarity through science, undermines the identity of science. We cannot call it a scientific reality, and if we use the term 'science' in such a case, it is necessary to indicate the one percent lacking, stating that our degree of guess and certainty has not reached the degree of real knowledge. The scientific claims of the nineteenth and twentieth centuries, especially in social sciences, later turned to be false. We shall mention examples of the issues which science, inspite of serious efforts, has not found yet.

We shall begin this discussion with two quotations from Camille Flammarion,[1] an astromoner, and Oparin,[2] a biologist, famous scientists:

> *You can see and you think, but what is thinking? No one has the power to answer this question. We take a walk; what is the essence of this muscular action? No one knows. We can see that my willpower is a non-material power; in fact, all my psychic properties are non-material. Whenever I desire to raise my hands, I can see that my willpower makes a material thing move. What is the truth of this happening? What is the truth of this medium which causes the execution of a usual command from a vital faculty? No one can be found who can answer this question. How do nerves transfer external images to the mind? How can the truth of this thinking be perceived? What is its agent [and not its scene of action]? What is the nature of mental action? I can ask you similar questions for the next ten years while the greatest mind cannot answer my simplest questions.*[3]

This is what Oparin says:

> *It is only through such evolutionary understanding that we can*

---

1. Nicolas Camille Flammarion (1842 – 1925): a French astronomer and prolific author. [Trans.]

2. Alexander Ivanovich Oparin (1894 – 1980): a Soviet biochemist notable for his contributions to the theory of the origin of life. [Trans.]

3. Muḥammad Far¢d Wajd¢, 'Al¡ A§l¡l al-Madhhab al-M¡dd¢ (On the Slumbers of the Materialist School), p. 38, quoted from Quww¡-ye Majh£l dar ±ab¢'at (Unknown Power in Nature) by Camille Flammarion (all originally in Persian).

possibly find the truth. Not only can we understand what takes place in the bodies of living organisms and why, but we will also be able to answer seven million 'whys' before us, for really knowing the essence of life.[1]

Definitely, if we add these questions "why movement must be evolutionary?" and "why evolution must follow this path?" to the abovementioned seven million questions, we will have seven million and two questions. Fortunately, Oparin himself has been aware of these two questions. In another place, he says:

Unfortunately, the information about this evolution has not yet reached the point when we can systematically determine its direction and pay attention to the quantitative changes in the structure of active transfer of cases which happened in specific stages of the evolution of the world.[2]

Erwin Schrodinger argues:

Without the existence of God, one cannot answer the question of the emergence of life, through an intellectual method.

He also said:

The basic elements of the living being are not an effect of a rude human (nature); it is rather a very subtle work done on the basis of certain principles of God's perfected quantum mechanics.[3]

In the introduction of the book, Life = Physics + Chemistry? Life from the Perspective of Eminent Physicists, Bernd-Olaf Küppers[4] is quoted to have said:

Man will understand the more important concept of the complexity of living systems when he organizes (elucidates) the abundance of possibilities (probabilities) of the basic structure of

---

1. Alexander Oparin, °ay¡t, ±ab¢'at, Mansh¡' wa Tak¡mul-e ¢n (Life, Its Nature, Origin and Evolution), p. 183 (originally in English).

2. Ibid., p. 299.

3. Erwin Schrodinger, Was ist Leben? (What is Life), p. 151.

4. Bernd-Olaf Küppers (1944 -): a German physicist, philosopher and theoretical biologist. [Trans.]

the hereditary molecule." [According to Pascal Jordan:] In a chain of molecules with four million basic structures, 102,400,000 different channels for complete organization can possibly be considered whereas the number of electrons that constitute the great universe is 10120.[1]

Now, we shall enumerate the questions which science has not yet provided convincing answers to in spite of incessant efforts.

1. What is the way of affirming the objective reality outside the mind, and in general, the way of affirming the "ego" vis-à-vis the "alter ego", pure science or pure scientific philosophy?

2. What is matter? Matter in its absolute sense is treated as the replacement of the sublime truths in the universe, and not as particular natural elements and phenomena defined according to specific stances and goals.

3. What is motion? What is energy and what are its parts?

4. Are the types of motion limited to the ones utilized by basic science and its derivative sciences?

5. What is the nature of relationship between matter and motion?

6. Why does matter move?

7. Why does matter move in a certain way?

8. Granted that the system of the universe is open, can it be said that the same motion in the same path is eternal or not? What is the proof?

9. Is the division of existence into objective and subjective beings based upon a rational foundation?

10. Is the real demarcation line between the "ego" and the "alter ego" specific, or is it a conventional demarcation line, as some authorities have believed about the fundamental particles in nature?

11. Since our knowledge and information is a product of the "ego and its faculties of perception", and the "alter ego and the conditions of the perceived object", what is the scientific basis of the claim that the mind reflects the objective realities without the

---

1. Life = Physics + Chemistry?, page. 26. (Original German text).

interference of the faculties of perception and conditions of the perceived object? Is it not so, as Laotzi the Chinese philosopher declared as quoted by Neils Bohr of Denmark that "In the great stage play of existence, we are both performers and spectators"?

12. Is the demarcation line between the "ego" and the "alter ego" in science and knowledge, absolute or relative? Granted that it is relative, what is the factor for its relativity? What is the quality and quantity of our pieces of information? Are they only the stances of the perceiving agent, or the perceived objects and our mentally preconceived principles?

13. Are the pieces of information and discernments that man acquires such as, bringing to fruition the seeds sown within his self, or are they acquisitions and reflections? Should the unprecedented mental activities be distinguished from the pieces of information, which are activated by means of teaching, learning, experiments, and observations? In the parlance of Westerners, are they a priori, or reflective, acquired activities that have no precedence within?

14. What is the correct interpretation of the abstract activities of the mind, abstract concepts of universal numbers and universal propositions, and their essential or accidental differences?

15. In case of stability of our necessary relationship between the laws of nature and the laws pertaining to human realities which are outside the domain of one's freewill and based upon realism, in which the necessity for laws of a reality is actual, not an abstract phenomenon, which is against this necessity which is a contingency. Is it possible that based upon the rule of changing thesis into antithesis or producing thesis out of itself, there will be a time when out of the interactive composition of the two elements of hydrogen and oxygen with specific amount, a sugarloaf or a train with twenty wagons will come into being? This question is asked assuming the invalidity of the theory of pursuit of event, according to the view of David Hume, and not considering all realities in nature proceeding from above nature, and the existing necessity among their laws related to the human

stance in the domain of knowledge.

16. Has the law of "the end justifies the means" any conditions, and is it absolute? Let us assume that it is conditional; will the scientific truths not become ambiguous? This is while scientific truths always talk about permanence in different ways and forms, although mental conditions, experiences and knowledge lead to different interpretations, and it is clear that difference in understandings is not identical with the ambiguity and variability of truths. For example, since the appearance of animals on earth, self-defense is the most all-encompassing principle in life, although two scientists or two philosophers may not arrive at identical answers to questions about the nature and essential and accidental peculiarities of life.

17. What is the exact and comprehensive definition of perceptible and intelligible beauty?

18. Does the real person have these two types of beauty (perceptible and intelligible)?

19. What are the causes of different reflections of the self in relation to colors [in individual or synthetic state, due to various combinations]?

20. Is there a direct relationship between abstract beauties to perceive the nature of beauty and man?

21. Is absolute abstraction in beauty and universal concepts and the substance of the view in general on this issue possible?

22. What is the definition of the essence of the numbers such as 2, 7, 100, etc. (apart from their figure, written and oral forms)?

23. What is the real and convincing interpretation of mystical disclosures and inspirations?

24. What is art?

25. Are scientific, technological and artistic discoveries and philosophical and ideological outlooks a kind of phenomenon?

26. To what extent are these phenomena conscious and free?

27. What is genius and what are its types?

28. What is the factor that makes a person remember a forgotten subject or case?

29. What is the definition of the nature of thinking and what

are its types? What is the difference betweening thinking and intellection?

30. What is corporealization (considering an existent as non-existent and a non-existent as existent, and acceptance of it in a given case)?

31. What is intuitive knowledge and the sense of contradiction felt for it (the unity of the perceiver and the perceived object)?

32. Is the rule "The general is bigger than its part" absolute or conditioned by qualitative limits?

33. There are many axiomatic principles, which are essential to observe in all human sciences and branches of knowledge. Are they limited to rational and absolute, or inductive principles?

34. What is the comprehensive definition of pleasure? Do the different types of pleasure, such as the pleasures of food, sleeping, knowledge, victory, and aesthetics constitute a single reality or diverse realities?

35. What is the comprehensive definition of pain? Do the different types of pain, such as physical pain, the sting of ignorance, the bitterness of defeat, and the displeasure of coming in contact with filthy items, constitute a single reality or diverse realities?

36. What is the way of knowing the main reasons for the emergence of civilizations, their exaltation and their fall, through the scientific method?

37. What is the cause of variation in the 164 definitions of culture?

38. What is the criterion of a purposeful and advanced culture?

39. Is it essential to coordinate all the elements of culture? With this assumption, what is the reason behind the incapability of man to coordinate them?

40. What is the reason behind inconsistency of the two great elements of culture, viz. human sciences and technology?

41. What is the ultimate definition of man?

42. Is the knowledge about man, without considering his moral aptitudes and actions, a complete knowledge? The basis

for this question is that anyone who knows that man has the aptitude for justice and serving his fellow human beings knows man better than anyone else who has no information about this aptitude.

43. Considering his moral aptitudes and activities, what is the impact of the knowledge about man in his movement for perfection?

44. What does make historical movement possible? Must this factor be definitely a reality?

45. Is the infinite mental perception a perception about quantity or about quality?

46. Is the infinite mental perception conceptual, actual or real?

47. What is the easier and more direct way of acquiring the principles and fundamentals of the universe, perceiving its orderliness, or its beauty and splendor?

48. What are the channels and means of the human beings' development from the realm of natural essence to the realm of ideal essence and then to the realm of the essence of perfection?

49. What is the way of solving and reconciling the two views on the world: infinite and finite?[1]

50. If our knowledge of the present condition of the universe is sufficient, what is the way of knowing its future condition?

51. What are sudden psychological upheavals and their amazing effects; are they for goodness or for wickedness?

52. What is the interpretation of sublime feeling about sublime duty?

53. What is the way of curbing the mental activities of some individuals which are not supposed to be destructive but supposedly constructive?

54. What is the definition of the phenomena of willpower and freedom and the ways of utilizing them?

---

1. Here, there are two contradictory reasonings: (1) the human mind cannot fathom the potential of the world; therefore, it is infinite; and (2) in view of determining the history of the big bang and the rule of generally following the implementation, on the basis of the limitation of every part which is of this type, it is thus finite.

55. How can the law of causation be reconciled with the voluntary actions of man?

56. What is the way of freedom from freewill?

57. What is the way of sublimation of the psychological condition of people apart from compulsory, emergent, involuntary, and reactionary actions and, in addition to voluntary actions?

58. What are the definitions and ultimate way of reconciling the phenomena of devotion (ta'abbud) and intellection (ta'aqqul)?

59. What is the ultimate way of reconciling the three concepts of power, right and falsehood, placed against one another?

60. We know that man is yet to regard power as justice, and powerful as just! Is there hope that, one day, tyrants will regard justice as power and just as powerful?

61. Will man be able to establish a free relationship with power in all its forms?

62. Does primacy rest upon the individual or society, and what is the way of determining the dimensions of their primacy?

63. What is the comprehensive definition of "money"? Is it possible to urge using money for good, or what is necessary? Or, will he not be able to ever do this vital task?

64. What is the real value of different types of action, such as physical, mental, or exploratory actions, actions that yield common outcomes, and those whose fruits are sublime?

65. What is the essence of memory and the status of its retentive powers, considering that a sound memory can store one trillion pieces of information?

66. If the pieces of information reflected from the physical forms are restored in the brain's memory, where are the formless and shapeless pieces of information, such as universal concepts, stored?

67. Has the bond of the body and soul reached its ultimate state, or will it always remain ambiguous?

68. Are the absolute concepts, such as absolute motion and absolute matter, a set of truths, or abstract and mental matters?

69. What is the comprehensive definition of perfection and excellence? It is said that logic never makes mistakes, and accordingly, it is imagined that the error of the scholars is traceable to their mistake in the application and collation of rules; otherwise, the rules by themselves are undoubtable. In the same manner, mathematical facts, according to general opinion, are derived from a set of axiomatic and undeniable propositions! And the same facts are so [seemingly] certain that not only us but even nature must abide by them and the same empirical laws can show us all the unknown aspects of the world... Yet, as the scholars and scientists reflected on, they found out that mere mathematical and empirical rules can never be sufficient to rely on. They said to themselves: "Are these preliminary points and principles sufficient for all we know, or can a puff overhaul these foundations? By relying on these principles and rules, anyone who doubts and denies is very superficial, and since doubt and denial does not require any reasoning, he makes himself glad!"[1]

70. Upon which transcendental cause is realism depended?

71. Excluding religion, from where can the answers to the sextuple fundamental questions be obtained?

72. What are the ways of making use of science for the sake of real benefit for all human beings?

73. What is the essence of time? Is it a subjective reality or concrete-objective reality?

74. Do we have a way for humanity to make use of the sublime blessings of realistic modernism and innovation?

75. Is there a way out of the three claws of time (past, present and future)? What is that way?

76. Is time a reality? Does it have types and parts such as physical time, psychological time, cosmic time, etc.?

77. What is the scientific validity of presenting life, soul, existence, and personality as the given properties of the specific system of matter?

---

1. 'Alī Aṣlịl al-Madhhab al-Mịddẹ, vol. 1, pp. 134-135 (originally in Arabic), quoting Science and Hypothesis by Jules Henri Poincaré.

78. What is the scientific validity of the proposition that all things consist of a unity?

79. Does the division and breaking up of particles continue ad infinitum? Given the limitation of every particle, how is this division and breaking up possible? If this division or breaking up stops for a moment, for instance in basic particles like electrons, how is it possible for a thing to maintain his physical continuity (even in the smallest possible extent) and not be divisible and separable (anymore)?

80. What is the essence and value of experiment and observation in science?

81. Is the restriction of all channels of looking for the truth in pure science scientific, philosophical, or neither scientific nor philosophical? Is it not pure imagination?

82. What is the essence of science?

83. What is will or will power? How can [physical] actions, which are effects of non-physical will power, be interpreted? What is the boundary between action and will power?

84. Freedom of belief means to have or not to have belief in what or whom, from the perspective of human values?

85. How can neurons transfer external forms to the brain?

86. What is the nature of the phenomena and mental activities?

87. What does this statement, of the famous mathematician Henri Poincaré, mean: "Scientific truth from the perspective of the common observer is far from any sort of doubt and scepticism, and he imagines this element"?

88. Is the relativity of time an intelligible truth?

89. How can realities be divided in this manner: "a thing for itself, a thing for us, and a thing in the affair itself"?

90. What does this statement of Descartes mean: "If a person allows himself to doubt the existence of God, he cannot prove to us even the most axiomatic mathematical statement like 2 + 2 = 4"?

91. With the negation of God and eternal life, how can one explain the human motives for acquisition of virtues, sublime morality, selflessness, and self-sacrifice along the way of human

ideals?

92. How can those schools of thought that present themselves as defenders of humanity justify themselves through scientific rules, whereas humanity and its defense, vis-à-vis the notion of the survival of the fittest, is emotional and perceptual?

93. Can humanism be proved vis-à-vis the notion of survival of the fittest?

94. What is the way of reconciling matter and spirit in the logic of science and human life?

95. Is the movement of man and the perpetual development in his life and history evolutionary? Of course, evolution here means conscious free movement and development. Does this evolution follow a straight line?

96. Is the value of four types of freedom, viz. freedom of belief, freedom of thought, freedom of expression, and freedom of action, absolute? Or, does it depend on which proposition, reality or objective it is applied to?

97. Is it proven by science that our knowledge and learning does not encompass a more expansive and meaningful world? We know that a number of scientists and philosophers believe that the world of nature in which we live is encompassed by another world possessing a higher reality and principles. They are William James[1] and Bertrand Russell, who are most indifferent to metaphysical and supernatural reality.

Max Planck has indicated this point in the books The Image of the World in Modern Physics, and Where is Science Going? Oswald Külpe has also agreed with the abovementioned point. Einstein also acknowledges the surprising limitation of physics, particularly in terms of the limitations of the tools of perception.[2]

98. Is the system of the universe open or close? Does, what is behind the concrete and perceptible, also pertain to the same realities, which we can see in the world of nature.

---

1. 'Al¡ A§l¡l al-Madhhab al-M¡dd¢ (On the Slumbers of the Materialist School), p. 135, quoting the book Ir¡dah I'tiq¡d (Willpower - Belief) by William James.

2. Bertrand Russell, The Concept of Relativity. (Originally in English).

99. Many of the propositions—especially in social sciences— are considered scientific, whereas their proofs of scientific verification are insufficient, but they are brought forth and defended by some individuals according to certain tastes and goals. What is the way of solving this harmful issue? That is, if we assume that proving a proposition as a scientific proposition with a hundred degrees of discovery and connection with reality requires ten percent or higher to be scientific. In this manner, a kind of uncertainty in the scientific discussion and investigations will be generated, and the egoists take advantage of these situations all the time.

100. Can the claim of scientists about scientific issues be the definite criterion and proof of their validity? The answer of the wary thinkers to this question is negative.

> Science is nothing that can teach us the total system of the universe. It is only a handful of ambiguous identifications. We do not know a considerable number of stars in the cosmos. So, any assumption or opinion we express about the system of the universe is futile and a claim bereft of any proof. The conservative natural philosophers do not accept that their views about the heavenly bodies are nothing but fiction! If natural philosophy is not a belief above the domain of science, then what is it? Does the world of nature [in a sense only] say what it knows and identifies? Or, does it go beyond that? No! Did the chemist identify [all] the components of life? How did he prove the generation of solids? Have the principles of the philosophy of growth and progress been perfected and freed from any kind of turbidity? Has the theory of matter and power reached its ultimate state? Have the scholars arrived at a consensus of opinion on all the subjects of their discussion? Is there still room for debate that the system of the universe is perpetually subject to laws? Yes, it is possible for a scholar to answer these questions but his answers will not exceed beyond the limits of a handful of speculative beliefs which are only preferential in nature. But the natural philosophers are so confident in relying on these unscientific beliefs that it is as if these are everlasting rules,

whereas the best and most unwavering scientific law is still doubtful for us, and no one can prove its being essential, just as its falsity cannot also be established! In a nutshell, we must say that natural philosophy is replete with unestablished views which can never be established even in the end.[1]

101. Must the principle that human beings always want to delve into the exterior aspects of things and know their truths, be continued? Or, must they be contented with the same phenomena and peculiarities in view of the fact that seeking for the truth leads to the advancement in science and technology?

102. When some extreme positivists claim that "All religious propositions are meaningless," have they explained what they mean? When they encounter this proposition: "If there is no eternal life, we must say that life only revolves around the axis of the powerful; none of the sublime values of humanity can be proven; anyone powerful who observes the rights of others and takes a step along the path of human felicity is the most foolish of people!" Do they consider it a meaningless proposition? When religion states: "Along the path of intelligible life, look for the answer to the lofty objective of life." Is this a meaningless proposition?! When religion maintains: "The ardent desire to search for perfection which is in you will not be satisfied except by being situated in the Axis of Absolute Perfection." Is this a meaningless proposition?!

103. Positivism holds, "Only the following are meaningful propositions: (1) empirical propositions which are built upon perceptible data ("Now, there is rain outside the room"); and (2) outward definitions, tautologies and verbal contracts (triangular). In view of the fact that universal laws and the immateriality of the soul as indicated by order, and the laws which prove the consciousness of the Supernatural Being as the universal cause, the positivists must answer the question: Why

---

1. Andre Cresson, The Rules of Natural Philosophy. (Originally in French), as quoted in 'Al¡ A§l¡l al-Madhhab al-M¡dd¢ (On the Slumbers of the Materialist School), pp. 139-140.

is proving such metaphysical propositions linked to "perceptible matters"?

104. Is there any hope of a time coming when man will find his lost "self" and commence his movement for perfection after knowing his real "self"?

105. Will man be able to find the appropriate subjects and items for physical, mental and emotional endeavors as well as his intelligence, visualization and will power?

106. Will man realize in the near or distant future that he should consciously and freely organize his four types of relationship?

107. Is it not positivism, which makes the weapon of mass destruction a winner, under the pretext that "Respect and honor for human lives is not a meaningful proposition but rather a personal moral understanding"? Did it not make the egoistic and powerful dominate the rest of humanity?

108. If the criteria for science and reality are sensory perceptions and experience, that is, in the words of Barbour,[1] according to the positivists "Only the experimentable propositions and definitions are meaningful,"[2] then what kind of proposition is the totality of this universal proposition, which is not derived from perceptible and empirical data?

109. Is the question of memory (not determining its place in the brain) which means the possibility of containing a trillion units, resolvable, in view of the fact that the human brain cells do not exceed seventy million?

110. Usually, wherever man is the one involved, there is always the possibility of misuse of the expressions, way of thinking, intellection, freedom, and moral concepts, for man is unlike other creatures that cannot stand against influential factors and neutralise their effects within themselves. Man may

---

1. Ian Graeme Barbour (b. 1923): an American scholar on the relationship between science and religion. [Trans.]

2. Ian Barbour, 'Ilm wa Dīn (Issues in Science and Religion), trans. Khurramshīhī, p. 280.

commit a crime and resist for years, nay throughout his life, against the factors that may lead to the disclosure of the crime, never allowing it to be exposed. Is there a way to prevent this misuse?

111. What is the ultimate solution of "Art for the sake of art, or art for the sake of man's intelligible life?" "Science for the sake of science, or science for the sake of man's intelligible life?" and in general, every desirable phenomenon or activity which can be taken away from man and become valuable only to its usurper?

112. Can the existence of universal and inalterable laws in science and philosophy make the universe and its processes be needless of God?

113. What is the correct scientific explanation of the transformation of lifeless materials into living creatures?

114. Is the mental abstraction of the sociologist, (in a bid to perceive pure realities) from preconceived ideas and biases, caused by the environment?

115. How does the fusion of knowledge and values occur in scientific knowledge and regulation?

116. What is the convincing interpretation of the principle of action and reaction in the sphere of life, such as injustice, whose repercussion is in the offing for its doer?

117. How can we unify or coordinate religion, science, philosophy, ethics, and mysticism, and if it is impossible, how should we interpret personalities like Ibn Sīnj and Khwjjah Na¥īr al-Dīn al-±ūsī who held such ideas in the highest degree possible?

118. Is there a law available to the human being to prevent him from going to extremes? What is that law?

119. How can we harmonize order in social life with the granting of freedom, the ardent desire for which overflows from within, and suppression of which makes man consider himself as part of a lifeless machine?

120. What is the way of arousing the conscience and keeping it awake?

121. Is it possible to stir one's will power to put sublime human virtues into action?

122. We all know that all the eminent prophets, religious leaders, righteous rulers and upright moral figures have a consensus of opinion that man's love toward his fellows is beyond necessary transactions. Yet, what usually happens is, that out of necessity, a person gets closer to another person, and due to personal interests, he separates from him! Is there a way of applying this lofty principle?

123. What is meant by the philosophy of history other than the overall stimulating agent of history? Is there a way of initiating any change to it?

124. Is it possible to determine the rational limits of profiteering, pleasure-seeking and domineering?

125. In what way do we falsify the harmful notion that, human virtues and values are only meant for organizing social life, and they have no real essence?!

126. Is the classification of philosophy according to (1) the difference in periods (for example, Greek, Middle Ages and contemporary philosophy), (2) schools of thought, and (3) regions/continents a superficial or realistic classification?

127. Awareness is the most desirable state of the human mind such that a great figure like Mawlịnị (Rūmī) says, "Whoever is more aware has a strong spirit" while unconsciousness is tantamount to lifeless living! Be that as it may, what is man's illness that in most cases, he wants to escape from awareness? It is as if awareness is his enemy, and in the words of Mawlịnị,

> All the (people in the) world are fleeing from their free-will and [self]-existence to their drunken (unconscious) side.[1]

***

> They are fleeing from selfhood into self-lessness either by means of intoxication or by means of (some engrossing) occupation, O well-conducted man.[2]

***

> In order that, for a while, they may be delivered from sobriety

---

1. Rumi's *Masnavi*, Book 6, line 224.
2. Ibid., line 227.

(consciousness), they lay upon themselves the shame of wine and minstrelsy.[1]

Elsewhere, he says,

Since consciousness is the inmost nature and essence of the soul, the more aware one is the more spiritual he is.[2]

***

The demand of the soul, as of the heart, is consciousness. Whoever is more conscious, his soul is stronger.

Awareness is the effect of the spirit; whoever has this in excess is a man of God. As the world of the soul is entirely conscious, whoever is lifeless is devoid of knowledge[3]

In our era, which is better known as the era of science and technology, this unconsciousness has reached an astounding proportion, so much so, that if the various means of amusement are removed from human life, man will put an end to his life. Should something be done about it or not? What is it?

128. Will the day come when love and affection, which enliven the human spirit, re-enter the arena of human life and these stupefied unconscious creatures come to life again?

129. If alienation from the self and others is contrary to the law of human existence, then what is the way of proving the necessity for self-knowing and self-building?

130. We know that an overwhelming majority of people, due to incapability to curb egoism, live with "a virtual self". For this reason, whenever man is given consciousness, he treats his existence as devoid of the "real self". Shall we take a step to deliver man from life with "a virtual self"? Or, shall we leave him to himself to plunge into alienation from his self and others?!

131. In order to prevent power-worship, which may exist in everyone, can one think of a way not to formally recognize the life of anybody except that which is subservient to his will power? What is this way?

---

1. Ibid., line 225.
2. Ibid., line 149.
3. Ibid., line 150.

132. Can one prove through scientific laws the correctness of a policy, which the human beings have adopted for administering their social lives?

133. What is the real definition of democracy?

134. Has man been able so far to establish logical democracy in society? Or, since its real meaning is based upon the fictitious notion of "might is right," can democracy be implemented in its perfect form?

135. If man makes use of all the opportunities, mental or psychological powers, material and spiritual advantages, which he had lost due to selfishness and self-centeredness along the path of curbing egoism, where will he reach in his journey to perfection? Should we not seriously think about this issue, and what the outcome will be if we do?

136. Mistake and error in assessing and understanding personalities by usually exaggerating about them deprive the people from truly benefiting from those personalities.

137. One of the plagues that corrupt human science and learning is derived from narrow-mindedness in exaggerating the value of a subject about which a researcher conducted a study and acquired valuable information. For example, let us consider the use of power in human history. There are historians who witness the serious impact of power in its common meaning, looking at the effect of power in outward defeats and victories, thus concluding that power is everything! If they consider the meaning of power as control over oneself par excellence, and that every injustice has a repercussion, which will be experienced, sooner or later, by its perpetrator, and that primary power in the absolute sense is the destroyer of power itself, they will not be convinced of the subject of their studies.

138. Most people have not yet gone above the level of "I as the end, and others as means," nor taken a step toward the higher level of "everybody as the end, or, all as means for a lofty human goal". They do not even want to understand the two dimensions of man (as both the means and end) and harmonize their lives according to this principle! Given this, what must be done?

139. Will man recognize any limit in destroying his life for the sake of dominating others "in the name of technological advancement"? Or, will he even resort to mass murder?

140. Will man be able to solve the enigma behind the man-woman relationship, and rescue himself through his legitimate means from the sufferings and undesirable things caused by this enigma?

141. How can man's rivalry with others, and his inability to manage himself, be avoided?

142. We know that the method of analysis in social sciences undermines man's unity of life and soul. It is for this reason that we have been deprived of a real subject in social sciences. Now, what must be done so that social scientists would not be negligent of the unity of man's life and soul?

143. Usually, the dispositions that human beings acquire and with which they live make man negligent of his human identity. What can we do to uproot dispositions (such as judicial, political, artistic, and other dispositions) that prevent man from living with his human identity? Can one find a way that, while having one of these, man will not abandon his pure conscience and nature which constitute his original identity?

144. What is the impact of each of the hereditary factors, natural environment, social milieu, sudden psychological disturbances, and other deterministic factors upon the destiny of man?

145. The implication of this question is this: Can the quality and quantity of the impact of the said factors be determined? If the said factors impact human life, then how can activities related, training, education, and sudden psychological disturbances be interpreted?

146. Usually man's shameful incapability to find the truth due to wrongly thinking that the truth is antiquated with the passage of time, and, imagining that time is like termites that tear apart and consume any edible material; that is, time devours the truth, and, on the contrary, anything that appears today or tomorrow is an undeniable truth! What must be done to rescue

him in the actual domain of truths, which are vaster than the fictitious claws of time?

147. In social sciences, have the thinkers realized the truth that since the time when human beings have been deprived of faith that gives meaning to their lives or carelessly rejected it on account of present truths, they are always living in unknown tomorrows?!

My life fell victim to my tomorrows / Woe to this nowhere tomorrow of mine!

148. Has the dominance of machine over man reached a point when there is still hope to return human beings to their real identity, possessing sublime intellection, emotions and feelings? Or, is this hope totally lost and one must get ready to witness the total extinction of human identity? Since this hope is attached to the very firm roots in the soul, instead of effacing it, should one not make use of it in both arenas of theory and practice?

149. What is the effective and beneficial way of combating agitation and anxiety for the future, which is introduced as the illness of the 20th century?

150. What is the reason why the desire for worldviews, universal, philosophical and systematic insights, and pertinent realities has alarmingly decreased, and the views expressed are only sparks and fragmented propositions (though interesting sometimes)?

151. Will the day come when the individuals, who recognize themselves as deserving to administer human societies, and make promises to the people in a bid to occupy those posts, will fulfill those promises after taking charge of those posts?

152. What is the cause of inability of managements in realizing the reformatory programs and appropriate laws in constitutional laws, diverse rights, and ideal sociopolitical principles? With utmost clarity, Whitehead says, "Human nature is so complex and intricate that for the rulers, all the fixed and written reformatory programs are more insignificant than even the scratched and draft papers on the table for putting those programs into action."

153. How can we comprehend and state the relativities and

absolutes with limited and unlimited degrees?

154. Which are the constant and which are the variable? How can we determine their relationship with one another?

155. One of the most important intellectual issues is that the scientific movement, which needs to know both the analytical and synthetic methods, especially in the more general sciences, is defective.

156. Is there a way for nurturing sublime feelings for perceiving beauties, witnessing lofty truths and human emotions?

157. Are we certain that the realities of the universe as far as we know today can only be known through the scientific method and no other way?

158. Do the defenders of a mere natural life deny a life higher than "food, sleep, anger, and desire?" Should we abandon our children to be torn into pieces by the desires of the strong and merciless agents of nature, and not savor the taste of knowledge, the goal of life, faith to value, and particularly, the taste of rational freedom? Will the outcome of our work be only to train our children to satiate the desires for power of the egoists?!

159. Are we certain that the disorders in the lives of people, suicides caused by ignorance, indigence, and curable mental disorders do not affect the lives of indifferent and powerful people?! Do you think one can find on earth the most powerful individual who will not be stupefied, cannot get weak and will one day consciously live in real happiness?

160. Is there a way for the leaders of societies to prepare the ground for the lives of people with all the potential they have? Can one just sit idly and witness the passing away of constructive institutions for human perfection and allow behavior to ignore hundreds of truths and realities of the human life, mind and soul, and pretend, like Sartre, that man has history but no institution?!

161. Can we accept the ludicrous notion, that the life of today's man, lost in the midst of limited pieces of information, baseless wants, anxiety, alienation from the self and others, is molded by the excellent personalities of the past—such as

Socrates, Aristotle and Plato in the West and F¡r¡bī, Ibn Sīn¡ (Avicenna), Ibn Khaldūn, Ibn Haytham (Alhazen),[1] Abū Ma'shar,[2] Mawlawī (Rūmī), Mīr D¡m¡d, and ⁻adr al-Muta'allihīn in the East?!

162. Have the principles and laws of pure natural life been able to determine the bounds of forbidden territories for human souls?

163. Can one conceive of a universal code of law and a global culture without globalizing the powers and virtues of life?!

164. The foundation of universal human rights as well as that of universal morality consists of the innate honor, dignity and nobility of man. By official teachings in universities in the world, of proving the principle of natural selection and survival of the fittest), formally or informally accepting the [Hobbesian] notion of "man is the wolf of another man", and affirming the Machiavellian principle of "the end justifies the means", can one put forth a foundation of universal human rights and morality?! Why has no step been taken to remove this contradiction?

165. In order to escape from the absolute, which is denied by a group of skeptics due to their failure to comprehend it, shall we not be entangled with infinite absolutism? For instance, is the one, who wants to deny God and eternal life, not compelled to regard as absolute all the propositions used to deny the comprehension of the absolute? In the words of Hugo,[3] "instead of a Universal Will, he has to establish an absolute will for every existent, and in doing so, he thinks that he has staged an

---

1. Ab£ 'Al¢ al-°asan ibn al-°asan ibn al-Haytham, known as Ibn al-Haytham, Alhacen or Alhazen (965 – c. 1040): a Muslim scientist and polymath who made significant contributions to the principles of optics, as well as to physics, astronomy, mathematics, ophthalmology, philosophy, visual perception, and to the scientific method. [Trans.]
2. Ab£ Ma'shar, Ja'far ibn Mu¡ammad al-Balkh¢, also known as al-Falak¢ or Ibn Balkh¢ (787 – 886 CE): a Persian astrologer, astronomer, and Islamic philosopher, thought to be the greatest astrologer of the Abbasid court in Baghdad. [Trans.]
3. Victor-Marie Hugo (1802 – 1885) a French poet, playwright, novelist, essayist, visual artist, statesman, human rights activist and exponent of the Romantic movement in France. [Trans.]

upheaval in human thought!"

166. Is there any hope of a day when the powerful egoists would not dominate others by shedding the blood of the innocent, annihilating the weak and helpless; and instead, fill the stomach of the hungry, cover the naked, and educate the people, who are burning in silence due to their lack of knowledge as their means of attaining supremacy?! Is this aspiration of the pure-hearted individuals for a day when the world leaders, instead of employing force in its deceitful forms to dominate people, would take ruling over the people's hearts as their motto, by respecting them and organizing their "intelligible life", and treat them with utmost reassurance under their management?

167. A thousandth of all those physical and mental powers which man has utilized to ward off the opposition of his fellow human beings has not been used in the way of preventing calamities and afflictions of natural factors. This means that the shameful massacre of people by their fellow human beings for personal interests cannot be compared with his difficulty or nature, and this comparison will never happen. In view of this, may we request those who allegedly advocate human perfection to define perfection for us?

168. There is no doubt that lying, pretension and deception are against reality—regardless of their desirable or undesirable effects. This is because an unrealistic expression of a piece of information contrary to the reality tarnishes a personality in the same degree of its opposition to reality, for the human being is a reality that takes the truth, and not falsehood, as the means of his task. If due to impotence, a person has no natural strength to resist his own immorality, then his conscience is put into the spotlight, and it cannot regard seven as zero, and zero as seven, unless all elements of perfection in his innermost being are ruined. However, political science, which teaches the most basic element of order and perfection of individual and collective intelligible life of human beings, is plunged in lie, pretension and deception. O Machiavellians! Are you certain that you have no historical and moral responsibility whatsoever? If you are

certain, where have you acquired this certainty? Announce it to the people. Let them be convinced and change their opinion concerning you.

169. We all know that among the feelings of people, a penchant and intuition for beauty has specific desirability. In the course of time, does this intuition evolve within human beings? Or, following the fading away of life's vibrance, it diminishes as well? Present some beautiful items to the youth of this generation and then present the same items to the adults. (Of course, with the assumption that these two groups are psychologically sound.) Then ask these two groups about the effect of those beautiful items on them and about their peculiarities. Will you see a small degree of improvement in the answers of the youth regarding their perception of beauty? Or, on the contrary, on account of being intellectually mature, will you get very profound, pleasant and refreshing answers from the adults? Why?

170. How can one scientifically prove the greatness and value of personality to the powerful egoists, and say, "Do not breach contracts by relying on fictitious and momentary power, because your personality hinges on your commitment"?

171. Are the criteria of the realities of life the essential and legal truths, which God has manifested through the nature, principles and rules governing it? Or, is the criterion of the realities this slogan "Since I like it, therefore it is the truth"? Through which scientific or philosophical method should we prove that the criteria of the realities are essential and legal truths, and not the slogan "I want it without any condition or restriction"?

172. We know that man's ability to adjust and adapt is of immense importance, for it is through this ability that, in the words of some thinkers, within 24 hours a just person can turn into an oppressor and an oppressor into a just person. Is there a way to educate and train people to utilize this ability along the path of goodness and perfection, or none? The necessity for employing this ability will become clear when, due to the lack of

correct training in most cases, the ability to be resilient in depravations is utilized.

173. Do you know of a way to decrease the people's satisfaction (without any reason and cause) and to increase their rational satisfaction and acceptance? In most cases, man lives with acceptance without any investigation and strives to attain the elements of his acquiescence. It is clear that blind acquiescence knows no condition. For example, man accepted slavery because freedom had not even entered his mind.

174. Has noble acquiescence which leads to individual and collective progress, been examined so far?

175. Is there a way to organize a group for the collection of common views and beliefs of prominent personalities of human society in a bid to reform their material and spiritual condition and to turn into constructive competitions the conflicts that undermine those beliefs and views? There is definitely such a way, provided that this group is immune from the hands of Machiavellians who advocate the slogan "The end justifies the means in the world of politics", and the circles, that open the horizon of the universe (in an open system) for the experts in science, philosophy and worldview, be founded vis-à-vis the Vienna Circle.[1]

176. Will the efforts to prove that modern human religion (humanism)—if ever it is worthy to be followed in all aspects— is half way to yield any result? Granted that this school can respond to man's relationship with his fellow human beings, can it also provide convincing answers to the other four questions? (Who am I? Where have I come from? What have I come for? Where am I heading?)

177. For the salvation of humanity, will the global leaders take the major step of proving that the primary doubts caused by ignorance are different from the constructive doubt and sublime perplexity, which is attained at very high levels of knowledge

---

1. Vienna Circle: is a group of early twentieth-century radically anti-metaphysical philosophers who sought to reconceptualize empiricism by means of their interpretation of recent advances in the physical and formal sciences. [Trans.]

and gnosis, by adherents of the path of truth?

178. Can sociology be promoted beyond the physical studies of societal phenomena, which are usually effects and draw the attention of the thinkers (sociologists) toward the causes of those phenomena? Does actiology also have rules of its own? What are those rules?

179. In this period of history, can we predict the future condition of mankind so that, if it is full of hope, we could welcome it, and if it is discouraging on account of disobedience, carnal desires and loss of values, we would not be hopeful?

180. Is it necessary for a renewed and comprehensive examination of the identity and value of the schools of thought and ideologies that deal with the human being?

181. Is there a way or ways to enhance the social sciences and to rescue them from inertia and degradation? What is that way?

182. Why don't the scholars and thinkers reexamine their writings and works in order to remove contradictions?! For example, given Freud's strong insistence on the primacy of sexual instinct and the need to satisfy it, are they aware that later on Freud said, "Satisfying the carnal desires without restriction leads to the weakening of the intellect"?!

What answer will he give to his conscience who says, "I am upset by presenting inestimable questions and I acknowledge this discomfort"[1] Which psychological ailment does he, who used to suffer from mental complexes and ailing allergy for spiritual issues, want to cure?

183. Has the authority of the intellect been proved? That the authority of the intellect should not be questioned is not correct, because all these conflicting beliefs and schools of thought that have emerged claim to be rooted in the intellect, dividing the people into hostile groups. If the intellect's authority were founded on reality, all these ideological conflicts and struggles would not have existed.

184. Do we have methods of identifying ignorance?

---

1. Edgar Pesch, Andeshehhi ye Freud (Pensee de Freud), p. 93 (originally in French).

185. Can one acquire information about all the elements of ignorance?

186. Without doubt, great personalities—given their diversity—have been very influential in discovering and stating the ways to man's material and spiritual felicity. We know, however, that for the same reason, prominent figures have been the support of people. Has there been so far a convincing criterion for benefiting from these personalities so that it could be sincerely introduced to the people, thereby preventing its misuse?

187. In the field of physics, up to where will the division of particles continue? Is it possible for it to continue ad infinitum? Granted that all of them are limited and finite, how is it possible for them to be infinite? And if this division is suspended at a given time, will it later exist in the concrete realm of physics? Therefore, this division must not be suspended and if it does not exist later, how will an existent be extinguished?

188. Has the truth of mystical unraveling, inspiration and intuition been lucidly defined so far?

189. Have the conditions of the abovementioned phenomena been accurately identified so far?

190. Which is more valuable in scientific methods, reliance on axiomatic principles or reliance on essential propositions? Or, is the source of the need to rely on the axiomatic principles identical with their essential correctness?

191. Is the definition of value and its types completely specified?

192. In formulating an intellectual system, can one sacrifice the truths for the sake of perfecting the system, which has been supported and defended by thinkers? For instance, in order to prove that the foundations of the different aspects of human life are sexual desires, economic inclinations or political activities, can one overlook the fundamental role of racism, culturalism, movements based upon power and religion, an endeavor in the way of preserving human values? That is, shall we leave man in the midst of the diverse thinkers and fragmented pieces of

knowledge to continue his scientific and philosophical life? Or, shall we say that it is essential to strive hard in order to formulate an intellectual system? Ultimately, it is not a closed system but an open one. In this case, one will not be able to conceive a school of thought which can determine man's duty in relation to the four types of relationship without kindling the fire of zeal in the human beings, with sound mind, to comprehend all aspects of the abovementioned relations.

193. Has atheism presented a proof to prove itself, or not? The reply is that the life which is not God-based is the life in the jungle, where the predator is egoism with its two basic pillars (profiteering and avoidance of loss), without the chain of order and law. On the contrary, all the solid proofs available on the existence of God, the Exalted, in addition to the axiomatic dictates of nature guide towards collective peace. How can we afford to discard all these proofs and then in lieu of God, point to a universal reality like absolute matter, which is much in need of abstraction and not God?!

194. Is secularism based upon scientific proofs, or is it a way of making the people indifferent toward serious principles of life? In order to justify secularism, political philosophers have dissected the human soul (as internal and external dimensions) and named it "science"!

195. Can secularism be responsive to all the diverse and conflicting desires of the majority of people in society, notwithstanding the fact that the majority of people are seriously inclined to religious life, if superficial obstacles, particularly the stupefying media propaganda, are removed along their way?

196. We know that since the time of Jean Baptiste Lamarck and Charles Darwin, this theory, which is anchored in empirical observations and comparative analogies, has entered the domain of science, holding that in the evolutionary process, some of the monkeys ended up as "homo sapiens". Much hullabaloo has been made to establish that this theory is scientific, to the point of manipulating political schools of thought. Some scientists with a weak voice questioned the bases of the said theory, being a

scientific issue. Yet, the appalling presence of free thinking and modernism manipulated by the opportunists and the fear of being stigmatized as reactionary and retrogressive, pervaded the scientific cirle and one dared to open his mouth and criticize the bases of the said theory. Let us consider this point:

It seemed that in the coming years, science will be able to explain, elucidate and expose to the public the issue of evolution in terms of its mechanism and manner.

Alas! After the death of Haeckel, science instilled these displaced hopes and extensive ideas, and as Dr. Singer[1] observes, "Nowadays, the works of the great prophet, Darwin, in Germany, are located in parts of the libraries to which people rarely go if ever the issue of evolution has still maintained its power and influence. On the contrary, the law of Yana, about the evolution of the fetus has lost its value, and it is only in recent years that scientists were able to form a set of real lineage for man."

Different chains of our connection between man and animal were gradually lost and their being fake exposed. The carved fossils and stones found in Spy, Belgium in 1886, Britain in 1887, Java (Indonesia) in 1890, Germany in 1907, France in 1908, and China in 1929, clearly show us that the present European race is of a breed of individuals who had high intelligence and many skills, and in terms of physique, did not differ much from us. These individuals are known as Cro-magnon humans. Prior to them the representative humans were individuals whose fossils were those of Neanderthal and discovered in La Chapelle-aux-Saints (France). Marcellin Boule (1861-1942), the head of human paleontology institute in Paris, published his complete descriptions of them in 1911. Prior to them were the Heidelberg humans (Homo heidelbergensis) and only their jaws were found in Mauer (Germany) and it is the oldest acquired relic of the real human ever available.

---

1. Charles Joseph Singer (1876 - 1960): a British historian of science, technology, and medicine. [Trans.]

Concerning the eras prior to it, for a long period there was no information ever obtained. Some were thinking that the bones discovered in 1890 by Eugène Dubois[1] in Java belong to the Pithecanthropus; that is, a specific being that is "a species in between humans and apes". However, as Boule mentioned in the1923 edition of his Fossil Men, no definite view was expressed in this regard. From 1929 onward, the Chinese scientist Pei Wenzhong, the American scientist Davidson Black (b. 1884), and Franz Weidenreich discovered near the city of Beijing a group of fossil specimens with close similarity with Pithecanthropus and named Sinanthropus. Many years after the said research studies, Boule revealed that both of them were beings of our height between the ape-like humans and humans of our period. Nowadays, it cannot be explicitly expressed whether man descended from apes or not. Some pieces of information which seem correct to some extent show that we have common ancestry with human-like apes.[2]

In another place, Pierre Rousseau says about the emergence of technology and the appearance of man:

The emergence of technology and appearance of man are perhaps a repetition of this worthless subject; this great happening, which has definite importance in the history of planet earth, will always remain covered with mystery in thick fog and perhaps its nature will never be known to us. We know very well that most paleontologists related it to at least one million years ago; that is, to the fourth geological epoch. The newest discoveries in the paleontology of the human race, instead of clarifying to us the history of this subject, make it known that the human origins are so complex and ambiguous and this ambiguity has so far increased.

---

1. Marie Eugène François Thomas Dubois (1858 – 1940): a Dutch paleoanthropologist who earned worldwide fame for his discovery of Pithecanthropus erectus (later redesignated Homo erectus), or 'Java Man'. [Trans.]

2. Tjrekh-e 'Ul£m (History of Science), trans. °asan ¯affjrd, pp. 650-651 (originally In Persian).

New discoveries, instead of simple and one-dimensional progress as imagined in the past, show numerous and multifaceted branches that had more or less come into being and existed for a while and faded away, and only a set of them survived and initially led up to Homo sapiens or the rational man and precursor of today's human being. Prior to this, paleontology maintained that today's human being is from the species of ape-like humans or pithecanthropus that came into being as a result of evolution of the Neanderthal man and then the Cro-Magnon man. Today, after vast and numerous discoveries in Europe, Asia and Africa, it has become clear that the obtained fossils do not belong to a specifically single species but rather to at least four different species, and our ancestor, that is, in reality, the ancestor of the 'rational' Cro-Magnon man is not the Neanderthal or Heidelberg man. And, we are neither from the predecessors of ape-like pithecanthropus humans nor from sinanthropus up to the genus prior to the 'rational man', whose fossils are absolutely unknown and unidentifiable.[1]

197. Is there a way of making the celestial goals and spiritual values of arts scientific? If ever there is, how can we benefit from it?

198. There was a time when the "three stages" [theory] advanced by Auguste Comte, in a bid to interpret and explain the human account in relation to knowing the universe, had been accepted by some authorities. After the passage of time and the emergence of realities contrary to Comte's theory, was this theory or belief set aside, or not? These three stages are as follows:

I- The Theological stage: In this stage, which is the oldest period, man would attribute whatever he would see in nature to the supernatural, such as the genie, spirits, and gods.

II- The Philosophical stage: In this stage, man had advanced in knowledge to some extent and looked at the world from a

---

1. Pierre Rousseau, T¡r¢kh-e ˉan¡ye' wa Ikhtir¡'¡t (Histoire des techniques et des inventions), trans. °asan ˉaff¡r¢, pp. 19-20.

philosophical perspective. The blossoming of philosophy in Greece and during the Middle Ages, just prior to the Renaissance, belongs to this stage.

III- The Pure Science stage: In this stage, on account of astounding advancements, man established contact with the objective realities through observation and experiment, and it can be said that this period started from the Renaissance onward.

Through a brief examination, the flaw and baselessness of Auguste Comte's theory can be revealed.[1]

---

1. Eight points of criticism to Auguste Comte's three stages theory:

(1) From one perspective, the first period of man's contact with the external world cannot be theological because the shift from the perceptible phenomena of nature to a level above those phenomena requires the faculty of mental abstraction which, according to the theory of evolution—of which Compte's theory is a derivative—is supposed to take place in the subsequent periods. And if we think that in that period man had been capable of turning a natural effect into a natural cause, it follows that man had comprehended the law of causation at that time, and this in itself proves that even during that time, man had a philosophical perspective of the world.

There is strong possibility that the case has been exactly the opposite. That is, on account of the primitiveness of man's worldview, the people during that period had more physical outlook because shift from one effect to a cause of the same type seems simpler and easier.

Granted that due to the lack of directly observing the causes, the people during that period would search for those causes behind the phenomena of the concrete world, this does not mean that they would consider the causes behind the phenomena as divine truths. That man regards phenomena in the physical world as metaphysical symbols is a common happening, which is prevalent even today. During that Theological period alleged by Comte, we know of schools of philosophy in the Indian subcontinent which are described as follows:

The emergence of philosophy of India: since there was not much attention given to history in ancient time, whatever shall be stated about the antiquity of Vedas and the history of Indian literature and philosophy is based upon speculation and estimation. What is obvious, however, is that philosophical ideas and moral goals appeared during the period of Upanishads and without establishing logical connection for a long time, they had remained in the same original state until gradually expanding and developing and forming the foundations, channels or principles of intellectual schools. The foundations, channels and principles of the philosophical schools of India are not a product of specific individuals' ideas, but rather a product of the ideas of numerous individuals who lived in different centuries in various vast cities and districts of this subcontinent.

After the formulation of different beliefs and ideas, some individuals engaged in

199. "Our account began with the question 'What is the tiniest particle of matter?' and 'Can we divide matter into its tiniest part?' and ended up with the discovery of the powerful atom consisting of orbital electrons and constituting the entire

---

learning, teaching and propagating the philosophical foundations while other individuals opposed the same, and there arose between these two groups disputes and debates as a result of which, the beliefs of each group have been polished.

Initially, philosophical ideas were transmitted orally from one person to another but have codified after sometime and remained from period to period. The pioneer scholars of India would present a subject in their gatherings and class sessions, establishing its validity or invalidity through criticism, argumentation and exposition. These discourses have been recorded with brief expressions called sutra, which are more akin to pithy aphorisms, allegories and allusions.

Philosophical schools: Philosophy in Sanskrit language is called Darsana. Most of the schools of philosophy that believe in the existence of God have maintained that through illumination the trained individual reaches Brahman (the Absolute Essence). The intellectual foundations of most of the philosophical schools of India are based upon the teachings of Buddha and Indo-chinese religions but they are beholden to this exceptional rule." See Upanishad, Sanskrit text as translated by Shₐhzₐdeh Muḥammad Dₐrₐ Shukₐh, son of Shₐh Jahₐn, with the introduction, marginal notes, glossary and edited by Dr. Tₐrₐchand and Mr. Jalₐlₑ Nₐ'ₑnₑ, pp. 51-52.

Then the author adds his points of criticism to Comte's theory thus:

Then we reach the Philosophical period, which according to Comte's theory constitutes the second stage. Regardless of the beginning of this period, it includes the period of flourishing of philosophy in Greece, Alexandria and the Middle Ages and in that very period, very important scientific figures among whom were Archimedes (circa 287-212 BCE), Euclid (323-283 BCE), physicians and even artists who were engaged in their activities with scientific affirmations of their arts.

Before generalizing his theory, how we wish Comte had visited the East and seen for himself how the Muslim societies, from the latter part of the second century up to the initial part of the sixth century, were engaged in their scientific activities through observations and experiments. It was already sufficient achievement that the Muslims rescued science from pure abstractionism by relying on observations and experiments during those centuries [which in the classification of Comte belonged to the Middle Ages and the Philosophical stage].

Comte is supposed to be asked, "On which basis can you prove that the number of philosophers after the era of movement in Europe up to our era (latter part of the 20th century) is lesser than the number of European philosophers during the Middle East? Can all these books and encyclopedias which reflect the ideas of European philosophers after the Renaissance period be ignored?!"

universe. The powerful atom, which is a great repository of energy and sometimes shakes in the boundless outerspace, producing waves in ether—exactly like waves in the pool before our eyes producing electrons and protons, and the waves of unknown ether are the materials that constitute the world. Today, what mankind knows, has not yet exceeded the least degree of knowing things. Great peaks in the territory of science still remained undiscovered. There are still dangerous paths ahead. Other planets are yet to be conquered. There are the works of those who want to enter the world of science and search for the ways of discovering the truth. This book only points out the adventure before us."[1]

John Langdon-Davies writes,

> *The physics of the power of its theoretical and scientific methods takes us closer to a single reality. This reality is very distant from the limits and boundaries of things perceptible. Once again, we recognize the greatness of the reality, which it is impossible to attain. These perceptions underpin the further perfection of scientific thinking (whose sequence cannot be severed and whose subsistence is perpetual).*[2]

Neils Bohr says,

> *Notwithstanding the incalculability of mysteries, basically such a question shall be posed in every stage of development of science, for every kind of scientific explanation is essentially to deduce a set of complex realities into another simpler set."*[3] *He also says, "We endeavor here to show the point that the efforts of the physicists are not in a bid to control this unparalleled situation by adopting the roughly intuitive stance of the biologists vis-à-vis the aspects of life. Now, let me point out that only because of*

1. Langdon-Davies, Shigift-h¡-ye Dur£n-e Atom (Marvels inside the Atom), p. 168 (originally in English).
2. Langdon-Davies, F¢z¢k-e N£: Tahawwul wa W¡zheg£n¢ dar F¢z¢k wa Falsafeh (Modern Physics: Change and Extinction in Physics and Philosophy), p. 17 (originally in English).
3. Neils Bohr, F¢z¢k-e Atom¢ wa Shin¡kht-e Ba∫har¢: N£ı wa °ay¡t (Atomic Physics and Human Knowledge: Light and Life), p. 17(originally in English).

this nominal observation that light, which is perhaps the simplest physical phenomenon, shows similarity to life whose analysis goes beyond the framework of the possibilities of scientific analysis.[1]

[Elsewhere, Neils Bohr also says,]

But in facing this problem, the conditions of research in biology and physics cannot directly be compared with one another because the need for survival of the creature under study exerts limitations on the research in biology — limitations whose similarity cannot be found in physics. For example, if we want to study the parts of an animal in order to determine the role of individuals in the vital functions of the animal, undoubtedly we have to slaughter that animal. It can be concluded here that any experiment done on living specimens is coupled with the lack of finality in terms of the conditions set on the living specimens under study. This matter prompts us to think that we forcefully give some freedom to the living specimens as much as is sufficient for them to disclose to us their ultimate secrets. From this perspective, the existence of life must be considered as a fundamental truth for which no amount of proof can be presented.[2]

Oppenheimer argues,

It can be assessed that real humans have always disrupted the efforts of physicists. Such things do not exist [in observation], and it is only by discovering them that physics can have access to its ultimate truth and reality, and can even go beyond that and believe that these pieces of wisdom relinquish the knowledge of other things including the science of physics itself.[3]

It is needless to say that most of the scientific advancements that took place in the 18th and 19th centuries soon complicated and set hurdles along the conflicting area between the giant-like

---

1. Ibid., p. 20.
2. Ibid., p. 28.
3. Julius Robert Oppenheimer, 'Ilm wa Farz¡nig¢ (Science and the Common Understanding), trans. A¦mad ¡r¡m, pp. 128-131.

machine and deep pit in the mind of the searcher, who had studied them and analyzed their characteristics. Such is the situation in the process of great statistical advancement which at the end of the day brought forth human ignorance as an explicit element in appraising the behavior of physical forces."

The power produced by science is a limited light in the midst of the unending darkness of human life and the world. Let us pay attention to the words of Oppenheimer, who presented for the first time the destructive power of the atom, practically for the extinction of the human race:

> We know that our work in reality is a means and a goal. It is a great discovery and an artistic work. With a firm and unflinching faith, we are aware that science in itself is good as well as a tool for replacements. It is a tool for branches of science, scientific arts and human affairs for researches and profound studies. It is for us as scientists and people. In the said unit, we are tools as well as the goal; inventors as well as professors; we are players as well as spectators. There is enhancement of skill. It is a word that has become so worthless. But, today, we anxiously witness that the power to execute changes does not necessarily bring about prosperity. Gradually, the new instruments of destruction and inciting collective fear become the means of increasing ferocity in an all-out war. One of the specific goals and issues of our time is harmonizing the eternal abode, improving the human condition, and uprooting hunger, poverty and misery with restraining violence, lessening resort to institutionalized cruelty among nations. Destroying the human soul in the most dexterous way possible through the police force which, if not more dreadful than the pillages against nature, it is more dexterous than them. It is one of the powers, which would have been, if not used at all. With this logical and just thinking, we say that society's support for science is mostly to enhance the power derived from science. If ever we want to utilize the power derived this way with wisdom and love for humanity, then approximately all other people also think the way we do. And we also know up to what extent the scientist can be aware of his expertise other than science, and of course,

he would not gain from acquiring it. Therefore, unity has both potential and actual state. And the terms of unity are things which, if put closer to one another, can lead one another to luminosity, and not collectively, generally, or consecutively.[1]

Even in science, and without entering into a foundation called atomic theory, all things are interrelated, thus calling to mind the complimentary features of our existence, particularly our professional life. Without the works of our predecessors, masters and contemporaries, we are nothing. Even when relying on our capability, talent and skill, we can have new understanding and system, we are still nothing in the absence of others, and with their existence, we become more than that. In our relations with the group in general, there is a similar duplicity and the reason for this is our work with one thousand meanings. It is a pleasure for those who continue it. It is training for those who perhaps need it. Yet, from another broader perspective, there is a common power and that is the materialization of something, which is impossible without science. It can be curing of an illness, relieving of pain and suffering, alleviating the inconvenience of the people, further expansion of the bounds of experiment and relations, and teaching in simpler language. We understand and hope that others would also understand that from this perspective, there is a similarity between science, which means specific universal pieces of information, whose goal is to discover, and human society. Like other people with less clarity, we enter into the vast and boundless darkness of the human life and the wolrd. For us as well as for them, change and perpetuity of stability, expertise and generalization, tool and ultimate goal, and the society and individual, that are complimentary, desire our commitment and freedom.[2]

---

1. Oppenheimer means that realities at the time of being situated side by side and benefiting from each of them for oneself and not as an organized group or individuals dealing with a general truth. Also, it is not such that some of these realities are at higher levels while the rest are at lower levels.
2. Oppenheimer, 'Ilm wa Farzₒnigₒ (Science and the Common Understanding), pp. 128-131 (originally in English).

The Effect of Preconceived Principles in Philosophical and Scientific Conclusions

It is true that, in view of the individual influence of the thinker, abstraction of ideas, from premeditated propositions and a priori perceptions, is possible. But, it must be borne in mind that the power that can withstand the influence of premeditated propositions and perceptions, or ignore or totally uproot them after being inculcated in the mind can only be found in a few individuals. Sometimes, this influence is so firm that it becomes one's second nature and its instructions like axiomatic principles, and each penetration into the pieces of knowledge is like the penetration of water into the roots, trunk, branches, twigs, buds, flowers, and fruits of a tree.

The penetration of a priori principles exists in both domains but is more effective in social sciences than in natural sciences. In general, these a priori principles and perceptions are of four types:

I. Correct principles and perceptions established by sciences, philosophies, axiomatic propositions, and essential propositions;

II. Incorrect principles and perceptions that cannot be established by acceptable proofs;

III. Principles and perceptions whose validity or invalidity cannot be established; and

IV. Propositions with both correct and incorrect properties

Correct principles and perceptions established by sciences, philosophies, axiomatic propositions, and essential propositions

As long as these principles are not related to science, they need not be absolute and eternal in all cases, because change and modification in scientific issues and principles exist, given the assumed openness of the inward and outward systems. For example, these circumstantial principles can be taken into account:

i. The need for managing life in both the individual and collective spheres;

ii. Truthfulness and justice for the realization of an "intelligible life" in the collective sphere;

iii. The necessity of paying the real value of goods and services as much as possible; and

iv. The effort to materialize the advanced culture anchored in genuine human needs.

Since such a priori propositions are present in every situation and condition, they are for the benefit of man's "intelligible life". As long as we can see that relying on such propositions does not harm our pieces of knowledge but adorns our life as human beings with the desire for perfection, we should abide by them.

Of course, it is the desire for perfection which thinkers in social sciences want to benefit from whenever they want, and invoke their correctness after reexamination. These renewed outlooks are not only limited to fundamental propositions but include new perspectives and accurateness in all principles essentially considered correct.

Incorrect principles and perceptions that cannot be established by acceptable proofs

The criterion of the falsehood of a proposition is that acceptance of it will lead to contradiction or inconsistency. An example of such false principles is as follows:

"In the domain of life, power always has the upper hand." If this a priori proposition is generalized on all categories of life, it will contradict the principle of necessity for preserving the values of a purposeful life. This is visible in the thoughts of Machiavelli and Nietzche. In items 3 and 4, you clearly witness the a priori principles of the wickedness, corruption and egoism of human nature. What will be quoted from Machiavelli in the next topics emanate from the same a priori principles and perceptions.

The political ideals of Machiavelli better known as Machiavellianism can be summed up as follows:

i. His purpose is the establishment of united, powerful, sovereign, and centralized Italian states that are not subservient to the Church and have far-reaching influence over Europe.

ii. Pessimism and support for injustice, despotism and unrestricted absolutist rule.

iii. Machiavelli argues that man is a political being who is by his nature corrupt, wicked and selfish. Thus, the absolutist state is required to establish order in society.

iv. Since people have been created wicked and selfish, the statesman must be, first and foremost, egoistic, and secondly, his policy must be based upon pessimism, violent reaction, harshness, tyranny unlimited. Since man is naturally aggressive, profit-oriented and insatiably desirous of increasing his wealth, securing his position, stabilizing his condition, and perpetuating his power, which are limited by nature, conflicts threaten society with sedition unless an overwhelming power prevents this and curbs these desires. The statesman is not only the architect of the country but also the architect of morality, religion, economy, and everything else. If the statesman wants to succeed, he must not be afraid of committing evil, because without doing so, it is impossible to preserve the state. Some forms of piety lead to destruction while some forms of wickedness bring about wellbeing. Only the state which relies on force is successful and nothing else. There is no available scale and criterion for judging the actions of the statesman except political success and enhancement of power.

v. Morality, religion and other social notions are all tools in the hands of the statesmen in order to obtain power, and these are not supposed to interfere in politics, statesmanship and administering the government.

vi. All rights and laws emanate from the statesman's administration. The statesman himself functions as the law and his stipulated law is binding, but he is immune from abiding by the law and morality, and the law can be abrogated and changed according to his prerogative. The statesman is above the law and can do whatever he wants. Morality is a product of the statesman's stipulated law.

vii. The government is anchored in the weakness of individuals and the individuals are in need of the state in order to protect themselves from other individuals.

viii. In order to obtain, enhance and preserve power, the

statesman can resort to force, chicanery, guile, treachery, murder, crime, fraud, and breaching of moral rules. No kind of action is ever forbidden for him, if it is done dexterously and secretly, if necessary. If he is accused of a crime or act of injustice, the outcome of the action, which is success, shall exonerate him.[1]

It is certain that if Machiavelli had not accepted "man's nature as evil and corrupt" as an a priori principle, he would not have unjustly left human beings in the claws of bloodthirsty rulers. Like other philosophers, sages and religious figures, he would have instilled the idea of justice and responsible freedom in the minds of rulers and leaders, and explained its ideal felicity to humanity. Since Machiavelli's a priori principle is totally against the essence of man, it follows that Machiavelli's ideas did not work. Neither was he able to hold a political position [again], nor create a sovereign, united and centralized Italian monarchy. Let's turn a sharp eye on the following passage:

We must consider this point just as the analytical political philosophy historians have done. By writing the book Il Principe (The Prince) and dedicating it to the then new Medici Pope (Giovanni), Machiavelli had also personal ambition, and through this book, he wanted to hold a political position again, through which the unification of Italy and formation of a unitary government in that country might be realized. Yet, neither was he appointed to any political position again, nor a unified Italy came into being during that century. Medici could no longer appoint Machiavelli to any political post, and at the same time, it did not possess the necessary conditions and power to bring into existence a sovereign, unitary and centralized Italian monarchy.[2]

Here, we shall briefly mention some political philosophers' assessment of Machiavelli's advice "to sacrifice all truths and

1. Bahi' al-Dçn Pjzjrgjn, Tjrçkh-e Falsafeh-ye Siyjsç (History of Political Philosophy), 3rd ed., vol. 2, pp. 432-433 (Originally in Persian).
2. Ibid., p. 436.

values as a means to realize the objective set by a statesman for himself":

> All the issues Machiavelli mentions in relation to political policy are based upon the assumption that human nature everywhere and at all times is basically selfish. The persuasive motive the statesman must rely on is indeed egoistic, i.e. based upon selfishness and self-centeredness, such as the desire to attain massive security and the concentration of power in the ruler... He again says, "Moreover, human nature has been created enormously aggressive and profit-oriented ...[1]
>
> Machiavelli's a priori principle lies in his failure to distinguish between "having" and "wanting" without which human life is unmanageable, and it is based upon "I as the goal and others as means", which leads to the utmost impudence and lack of remorse in the egoistic person vis-à-vis life, values and the rights of others! It is for this reason that a number of great philosophers have rejected Machiavelli's merit to express any view on political philosophy. It is said, Machiavelli's political writings have less philosophical dimension and more practical diplomacy and statecraft, and must be deemed diplomatic writings and not philosophical.[2]

Meanwhile, we shall witness in this very discourse the psychological impacts of Nietzsche, which have been derived from his a priori principle on the primacy of the desire for power:

> We have pointed out that during his student days in Leipzig, Nietzsche discovered the book Die Welt als Wille und Vorstellung (The World as Will and Representation) written by Arthur Schopenhauer, and although Nietzsche was pessimistic about it, it motivated him a lot in spite of his not being a student of Schopenhauer at all. In the Exoneration Tragedy, for example, he would look for Schopenhauer so that he could take something as his a priori principle, call it "eternal alienation", and manifest it in the world as well as in human life, and there, like

1. Ibid., p. 44.
2. Ibid., p. 436.

Schopenhauer, he led a dreadful and tragic life...[1]

The passage below by Nietzsche,explains his way of thinking after being influenced by Schopenhauer as his a priori principle:

> *In 1865 he gets a book by Schopenhauer, entitled Die Welt als Wille und Vorstellung. This book so deeply touches his soul that he says, "This book is a mirror in which I saw the entire world and life, nay the nature of the self (essence) in dreadful majesty." He seriously engrossed himself in studying this book, reading it with utmost enthusiasm and zeal. He says, "For me, it is as if I am Schopenhauer's addressee in this book. I perceived his epic feeling in this book and I imagined that in every line of this book Schopenhauer is standing, facing and shouting at me, "[If you can,] take an action to deny and destroy this book!*[2]

The very deep impact of the a priori principles upon Nietzsche's being [which is not supposed to be such] can be clearly seen. This self-defeatism to an a priori principle renders useless all values, human principles and other correct global rules, and with an "unimaginable egoism" it takes the future of mankind in its hand! Let us closely examine this passage:

> *Nihilism assumes various forms. For example, one of its forms is 'active nihilism'. That is, pessimistic submission and resignation to the effect of the vanishing of values and the aimlessness of life. But there is also an active nihilism that wants to break up that which it does not believe in anymore. Nietzsche predicted the emergence of active nihilism in the ideological wars which would shake the world: "Such wars which had no precedence on the surface of the earth will break out. It is only from my time onward, will there be so-called great politics!*[3]

---

1. Frederick Copleston, T¡r¢kh-e Falsafeh (History of Philosophy), vol. 7, "Az Nietzsche t¢ Fichte (From Nietzsche to Fichte)," trans. Dary£sh ¡sh£r¢, pp. 387-388 (originally in English a classic nine-volumes work on history of philosophy which has been wholly translated into Persian).
2. A¦mad Am¢n and Zak¢ Naj¢b Ma¦m£d, D¡st¡n-e Falsafeh-ye Jad¢d (The Account of Modern Philosophy), vol. 3, p. 512 (originally in Persian).
3. Frederick Capelston (?), T¡r¢kh-e Falsafeh (History of Philosophy), vol. 7, pp. 395-396.

The end of belief in the a priori principle, which Nietzsche proposed for himself and others, was the beginning of a kind of struggle against the self, which brought to him the following result:

> *Nietzsche set aside his plan until his violent attack on Wagner and writing of The Case of Wagner (1888) followed by Nietzsche contra Wagner (1888). This treatise along with his other writings in 1888 such as Twilight of the Idols, The Antichrist and Ecce Homo (which is a sort of autobiography) was published after his bankruptcy. Apparently, the writings of that year show the extreme tension and mental agitation he was experiencing, especially that a person at the peak of self-praise would clearly show. At the end of the year, definite signs of insanity were manifested in him and in January 1899 Nietzsche was brought from Turin where he was then living to a psychiatric clinic in Basel. From then on, he never recovered, but after some medication in Basel and then Jena, he was able to go to his mother's home in Naumburg. This became the fate of a popular person, though he was in such a condition that he could not comprehend it. Nietzsche died on August 25, 1900.[1]*

In this manner, the pages of life of a man ended along the path of proving the essence of power and power-worship, which he had allowed to dominate his mental faculties and activities. While passionately defending the primacy of power vis-à-vis the destructive contradiction between intellection and sublime human principles, and the a priori principle of "sacrificing everything, everybody, every principle, and every value before the altar of power", he buckled down in the most humiliating manner. The only lesson he gave mankind was: "Be aware and careful! By bombarding a baseless a priori principle, you must not initially take a step to wage an all-out war against human souls and then struggle against the self, and commit suicide!"

Principles and perceptions whose validity or invalidity cannot be

---

1. Ibid., p. 385.

established

These are like natural parts, divisible ad infinitum. These principles cannot be inculcated into the minds of wary and intelligent individuals who are well informed of the fundamentals of science and knowledge. Therefore, as pointed earlier, belief in and abidance with such principles cannot bring any harm to science and knowledge.

If the validity or invalidity of such principles has been established in advance it breeds concern if the one who believes in those principles—even invalid principles—has an outstanding personality in society, and portrays his a priori principles as established propositions. We may mention, as examples the names of Hobbes, Machiavelli, Nietzsche, and Freud. By finding the people's zeal of acceptance in every period, unfortunately, such people impose even their invalid a priori principles on the unwary.

Propositions with both correct and incorrect properties

The sensitivity of this group lies in the fact that distinguishing the correct and incorrect aspects is very difficult for most people, especially if the correct aspect is more attractive while the incorrect aspect is unnoticeable. The best example of such perceived principles is the same principle of power. Power in its different forms, is the administrator's most fundamental motivating element. It is power, which removes obstacles in life including natural and human obstacles. It is power, which brings into existence and enhances advancement in all its different forms. Power is one of the Essential Attributes of God; that is, the Regulator of the universe. On the other hand, it is power that causes selfishness and self-centeredness. It is power that tramples upon the rights of the weak, prompting its holder to treat the weak as such. It is power that crushes all human values and principles.

The ways to erase the effects of belief in the incorrect aspect of such principles are as follows:

i. Correct interpretation. Firstly, we must embark on interpreting and explaining the proposition. This proposition (a priori principle under discussion) is power. It can be said that power means the agent of motion and change. As we can see, this subject is the most basic agent of activity in the universe, human subsistence and the attainment of its ideal form. Given this definition of power, this subject is the greatest divine bounty given to human beings to make desirable changes in the realm of the universe.

ii. The manner of utilizing the principle has two dimensions, viz. constructive and destructive. Since the application of such subjects are related to the human "ego" (personality), if the personality of a strong person is wholesome and excellent, he is safe from the disobedience of the "natural ego", which has no motive or objective except circumambulating around itself and self-aggrandizement. Definitely, if he takes the constructive dimension of power as his driving force and never tramples upon the rights and lives of the downtrodden he should consider it as a victory for himself. And if one's personality is imprisoned by the power he acquires, obviously his "natural ego" will lay the foundation of disobedience and no principles, will be of any moment to him and he will extinguish them as sources of trouble.

The more the erroneous a priori principles influence human material and spiritual life, the more profound becomes their menacing harm. Such harmful principles are those of absurdism, the primacy of the sexual instinct, power-centeredness, and sacrificing every moral truth in order to attain a desired objective.

A Priori Principles can even Influence Natural Science and Philosophical Findings

This is possible to a greater extent in social sciences than in natural sciences because most fundamental propositions in social sciences are arrived at from what is conceived of man's being. Man's mental abstraction of the realities within him such as desire for power, selfishness, removal of weakness, perception of and inclination to beauty, utilitarian tendency, hedonism, triumph in competitions, desire for happiness, and abhorrence of sadness is a difficult task that requires power and personal wellbeing. It can be said that one of the most fundamental reasons for the decline in social sciences is the inability of most people to mentally abstract a priori principles that stem from racial, environmental and cultural factors as well as accepted general propositions. A priori principles in the findings of natural sciences and philosophy can be kept away on account of their being outside man's mind, psyche or "ego".

In view of human relations with the world of nature or the universe as a whole, and the limitation of scientific awareness, and instruments, and the openness of the system of the universe to be discovered, and the system of mental data and activities, it seems that we have two amphibolous principles:

i. There is no correct essential proposition except about which there is theoretical or reasoning proposition.

ii. There is no theoretical proposition except about which there is an axiomatic proposition.

For example, the proposition that natural particles are constituted of smaller particles is something axiomatic. Yet, concerning this axiomatic matter there are theoretical propositions such as these questions: Are these particles the same things referred to by ancient thinkers (such as Democritus) or the atomic particles put forward today by modern physics? Which of the diverse things put forward today is more acceptable? The answers [to these questions] are theoretical propositions.

The same is true with correct essential propositions such as this: every happening can be measured with a specific time. This is a correct essential proposition. Meanwhile, there are numerous theoretical propositions regarding time, happening and measurement. For example, does time have an identity? Is the origin of time the discovery of actual motion? Or, can inner motions also be the origin of the discovery of time? The same is true with the propositions related to happenings and measurements.

The question that "Does science have the method of finding

causative relations?" is as such a theoretical proposition. Born[1] argues,

> It seems that science has a method of finding the causative relations without resorting to any metaphysical principle. But this is a deception because no observation or experiment —no matter how expansive it is —can be repeated beyond a specific number, and the statement "B depends on A" always comes after experiment.[2]

We can consider here some axiomatic propositions concerning this proposition:

1. Science seeks to find a method for finding the causative relations.

2. Experiment is one of the means of acquiring knowledge of the realities.

3. Finding the relationship of cause and effect must be based upon general philosophical principles or a metaphysical principle.

From 1333 to 1335 AHS (1954-1956) While I was busy writing the treatise *Irtibịt-e Insịn-Jahịn* (Man-World Relationship)[3], the following question seriously drew my attention: As claimed by some thinkers and writers, is science not in need of general and philosophical principles, and do all scientific issues in all stages and dimensions emanate from pure scientific rules and laws? Hence, I examined and criticized this point to the best of my ability. The outcome of this examination and criticism which shows the influence of general and philosophical principles and rules in various forms is elaborately mentioned in volume 1 (pages 1-202) of the said treatise. The researchers may refer to the

1. Max Born (1882 – 1970): a German-born physicist and mathematician who was instrumental in the development of quantum mechanics and won the 1954 Nobel Prize in Physics (shared with Walther Bothe). [Trans.]

2. Gulshan¢, Ta¹l¢l¢ az D¢dg¡h-h¡-ye Falsaf¢-ye F¢z¢kd¡n¡n-e Mu'¡¥ir (An Analysis of the Philosophical Viewpoints of Contemporary Physicists), p. 226 (originally in Persian).

3 This monumental cosmo-anthropological work of Allameh Jafari has been edited and published by AJI in Tehran. Allameh has cited more than 1000 works ın this work and this shows his mind-boggling bibliological knowledge (Ed.).

said source. In 1369 AHS (1990) a treatise entitled Taḥlīlī az Dīdgᵢh-hᵢ-ye Falsafī-ye Fīzīkdᵢnᵢn-e Muʻᵢ¥ir (An Analysis of the Philosophical Viewpoints of Contemporary Physicists) written by the esteemed scholar Dr. Mahdī Gulshanī was published. In terms of references and research, this book is well written. Through incessant efforts and sincere studies, in this book the respected author has lucidly put forward important issues in modern theoretical physics and the influence and encompassment of philosophical viewpoints of modern physicists. This book is indeed an excellent scientific and philosophical breakthrough for the students of philosophy and physical sciences in the universities and seminaries. All the topics that the erudite author has dealt with in this book are very significant. Among these topics, what is directly related to our discussion is this question: Can physicists dispense with philosophy? It is hoped that the esteemed researchers consult it for further study.

Allameh Muhammad Taghi Jafari

(1923-1998)

About the Author

Muhammad Taghi Ja'fari (born 1923, Tabriz, Iran, and died 1998) was a contemporary sage and an expert in philosophy and Islamic knowledge. Ja'fari was familiar with Western culture and also with the needs of modern human being and the contemporary culture. He was indeed an original and innovative thinker.

One of the most important innovations of this honorable master was that he, like Allameh Tabatabaei and Sayyed Muhammad Bagher Sadr, used the methodology of comparative studies for introducing Islamic knowledge to a generation who was thirsty for truth. Indeed, Ja'fari has left us a collection of invaluable works on Islamic teachings, philosophy of arts, aesthetics, literature, mysticism, the study of the *Nahjulbalaghah*, psychology, human rights and pedagogy.

In addition to being an expert in philosophy, in Islamic mysticism and in *Fiqh* (jurisprudence), Ja'fari was familiar with the works and the ideas of classical Western philosophers such as Socrates, Plato, and Aristotle. He was also versed in the works of modern philosophers including Descartes, Leibniz, Hume, Kant, Hegel, and contemporary philosophers such as Balzac, Dostoevsky, Tolstoy, Hugo, and modern-day physicists including Max Planck, and Einstein.

Ja'fari's epistemic geometry comprises of the knowledge of the mind, the revelation and the heart, tradition and modernity, physics and metaphysics, law and aesthetics. While the first three sources were the main pillars of his thinking, the expressions of his thoughts were nonetheless the result of dialogues made on the different bases of this epistemic geometry, which – due to their up-to-date nature – made his works novel and attentive to the debates on the difficulties of the "modern human" and the "modern life".

Ja'fari's 15-volume *Rumi: the Man and His Ideas, an Interpretation, Criticism and Analysis of Rumi's Masnavi* and his 27-volume *Translation and Interpretation of the Nahjulbalaghah* have a distinct place in his body of work. In terms of the clergies' principles, attending to Rumi's *Masnavi* was a heresy, or disliked to say the least. Moreover, writing commentaries on the *Nahjulbalaghah* was considered as a virtue, not a science. Scholarship was, and still is seen as footnoting on important books on *fiqh* (jurisprudence). It was in such an environment that the honorable master instilled *Masnavi* back in the minds of students and academicians. By comparing Rumi's sublime and amorous assertions with those of French and Russian thinkers and scholars, with whom Iranian intellectuals are more familiar, he once again took Rumi's *Masnavi* back into Iranian homes, in which households were more acquainted with Western culture. Afterwards, by writing an exegesis on the *Nahjulbalaghah*, entitled "A Manifesto on Wisdom, Mysticism and Politics," he familiarized the younger generation with an Islam devoid of superstition, factionalism and backwardness, an Islam based on the mind, revelation, justice and love. We can consider Ja'fari as the vanguard in writing commentaries on Rumi's *Masnavi* and the *Nahjulbalaghah* in the contemporary era, to whom all the later commentators are indebted.

According to Allameh Ja'fari, love and the mind are the two wings that make humans fly towards the absolute truth. The mind and revelation, science and religion, the mind and *shari'a* (Islamic law) are all compatible and do not contradict one another. Of course, the mind is the solid pillar of knowing (episteme). In his thoughts on the political principles of Islam, he saw justice, compassion, mercy, tolerance, serving the people, and reliance on consultation (*Shura*) and also on people's decisions as the basis of Islamic governance.

In terms of personal character and ethical manner, despite his high stature, Ja'fari was humble and modest. Unlike some learned scholars, he did not consider himself as someone who knew everything; there was no trace of arrogance and contemptuousness in him. Throughout his productive life, he preferred the trappings of science by devoting himself wholeheartedly to the cultivation of intellectual life.

He passed away on 15 November, 1998 suffering from a cancer disease in London. He was buried in Dar-Al-Zohd, by Imam Reza's Holy Shrine in Mashhad.

The Allameh Jafari Institute

www.ingramcontent.com/pod-product-compliance
Lightning Source LLC
Chambersburg PA
CBHW051624120626
46551CB00014B/1932